DISCOVER CANADA

Newfoundland and Labrador

By Marian Frances White

Consultants

Desmond Morton, FRSC, Professor of History,
University of Toronto

Alice Collins, Ph.D., Faculty of Education,
Memorial University of Newfoundland

James K. Hiller, Ph.D., History Department,
Memorial University of Newfoundland

 Grolier Limited

TORONTO

Spaniard's Bay
Overleaf: **Norris Point, Gros Morne National Park**

Canadian Cataloguing in Publication Data

White, Marian Frances, 1954–
   Newfoundland and Labrador

(Discover Canada)
Includes index.
ISBN 0-7172-2715-4

1. Newfoundland — Juvenile literature. I. title.
II. Series: Discover Canada (Toronto, Ont.).

FC2161.2.W55 1993   971.8   C94-930094-2
F1122.4.W55 1993

Printed and bound in Canada.
Published simultaneously in the United States.
1 2 3 4 5 6 7 8 9 10   DWF   99 98 97 96 95

Front cover: Herring Neck, one of many small
   outports in the Twillingate area, on Notre
   Dame Bay
Back cover: Labrador's Kaumajet Mountains

The central part of St. John's, which has changed little over the years

Table of Contents

CHAPTER 1

Drifting Ashore

Many things set Newfoundland and Labrador apart from the other Canadian provinces. Water, of course, divides Newfoundland itself from the rest of the country. History also sets it apart since it was for so long a separate political entity. And, not surprisingly, isolation has produced a culture that is its own unique blend of Old World, North American and home-grown views and ways.

To tell the story of Newfoundland and Labrador is to tell of Native people who lived on the land long before written records were kept. It is to tell of Europeans who came to fish and then explored and settled the island, of pioneering families, of pirates, merchants and missionaries, of shipwrecks that still haunt the jagged coastline.

It is also a story of fishing, forestry and marine technology, of drilling for oil and gas, and of building huge hydroelectric plants. Across the province, people work in many different jobs — on blueberry farms and in salmon hatcheries, in government offices, tourist camps, research labs, and in a craft industry that is second to none.

With its topsoil scraped from its surface thousands of years ago by glaciers, the province is affectionately known as "The Rock." Its lifestyle was born of the sea over hundreds of years — and now it is changing with the tide as the fishing industry draws in its nets. In spite of hard times, this is a place of good humour, lively entertainment and exciting artistic creativity. It is a place that treasures its past even as it welcomes newcomers and adapts to new ways. Above all, it is a place where the inhabitants try not to forget that the real wealth of a province is in the resourcefulness of its people.

Waves crash on the rocks at Cape St. Francis, the northeastern tip of the Avalon Peninsula.

CHAPTER 2
The Land

With 568 475 residents, Newfoundland and Labrador is the second least populated Canadian province — only Prince Edward Island has fewer people. At the same time, its total area of over 400 000 square kilometres (154 000 square miles) is greater than that of the other three Atlantic Provinces (New Brunswick, Nova Scotia and Prince Edward Island) combined. There are two very distinctive parts to the province: the island of Newfoundland, where most of the population lives, and Labrador on the Canadian mainland. Thanks to countless deep bays, fiords and inlets, the two parts together have almost 30 000 kilometres (20 000 miles) of coastline. Cape Spear, near the capital, St. John's, is the most easterly point in North America and is closer to Warsaw, Poland, than it is to Vancouver, British Columbia.

The Island

The island of Newfoundland is roughly triangular in shape, with an irregular and dramatic coastline that includes many peninsulas and hundreds of bays. Cape Norman, on the most northern edge of the Great Northern Peninsula, looks like the tip of a pointing finger. Cape Ray at the southwest corner faces Nova Scotia across the Cabot Strait. Forming the island's southeast corner is the sprawling Avalon Peninsula, which is attached to the rest of the island by a very narrow strip of land.

Western Brook Pond — which would be called a lake by any but a Newfoundlander — and the Long Range Mountains

Topography

While Newfoundland has no mountain ranges to compare with the Rockies in western Canada, the island boasts some of the most striking scenery to be viewed anywhere. The Long Range Mountains, the island's highest, stretch up the west coast, along the Great Northern Peninsula. From 800 metres (2600 feet), the land drops dramatically into the Gulf of St. Lawrence. The south and east coasts are lower-lying, but remain generally rugged, with many hills and steep cliffs. Most of the interior is rolling plateau.

The island as we see it today was shaped over millions of years by the wrestling forces of volcanoes, moving continents and ice ages. Eons ago, the Great Northern Peninsula was a part of the mainland, and the Avalon Peninsula was attached to North Africa. During the last ice age, more than 10 000 years ago, moving sheets

Below: **Ice floes from the Arctic fill the harbour at Twillingate on Notre Dame Bay.**
Right: **Steady Brook Falls in the lushly wooded Humber Valley, just upriver from Corner Brook**

of ice scraped away most of the island's topsoil, leaving very little land suitable for agriculture. However, the soil dumped onto the sea bottom helped create fertile fishing banks and make the Continental Shelf around Newfoundland an ideal habitat for a wide variety of sea life.

Water

The island has thousands of lakes and rivers, most of them quite small. The larger ones are used for sports fishing, but more importantly they have contributed to the development of the province's natural resources. Water from Grand Lake in western Newfoundland is channelled by canal to Deer Lake to make electricity for the Corner Brook paper mill. The forested slopes of Red Indian Lake in central Newfoundland have been a rich source of wood, and the lakes and rivers have been used to float the timber to the pulp and paper mill in Grand Falls, on the Exploits River.

The Exploits is the island's longest river. It rises in the southwest corner of the island, flows into Red Indian Lake and then northeastward to empty into Notre Dame Bay. The island's other main rivers are the Gander and the Terra Nova in the northeast and the Humber in the west.

Climate

The island reaches far out into the Atlantic Ocean, and its weather is therefore greatly influenced by the sea and by the Labrador Current, which sweeps down from the Arctic. In a general way, the ocean moderates the climate because it both cools and warms more slowly than the land. As a result, winters are a bit milder and summers somewhat cooler on the coasts than they are inland or in continental areas of similar latitudes. Spring comes late, however, because of ice brought south by the Labrador Current.

Newfoundland is known for winds than can reach as high as 180 kilometres (110 miles) an hour. On the west coast near Channel-Port aux Basques, an area has been named Wreckhouse because the

The fog-enshrouded wharf at Petit Forte, Placentia Bay. *Inset:* A lovely condition called *glitter* is caused by freezing rain. It is most noticeable in the early morning before the sun has time to melt the thin crust of ice on trees and shrubs.

high winds have blown Canadian National trains off the track. The wind can also shift direction very suddenly, creating an abrupt change in the weather. Newfoundlanders like to claim that you can experience all four seasons in a single day on the island.

The average yearly rainfall in the capital city is 1147 millimetres (45 inches), and freezing rain is common in the spring. The cold Labrador Current clashes off Newfoundland's coast with the much warmer Gulf Stream, which comes from the south. The result is frequent fog that becomes thickest in June. However, at the same time as fog hides the sun along the coast for the whole day, the trees a few kilometres inland may be basking in warm sun.

Vegetation
The forests of Newfoundland have changed greatly in the 500 years or so since Europeans began to visit the island regularly. At one time, they grew down to the seashore around much of the island and included extensive stands of white pine. Today, only about 40 percent of the island is forested. After being repeatedly cleared, often by burning, most settled areas along the coasts are virtually

An exceptional display of autumn colours in the heavily wooded interior of the Bonavista Peninsula. *Inset:* One of Newfoundland's elusive bog orchids, the showy lady's slippper

treeless; white pine fell victim to a combination of disease and logging and is now relatively rare. The forests are thickest along the river valleys. White and black spruce and balsam fir predominate; birch, red pine, aspen, poplar and ash are fairly common.

Many flowering plants are indigenous to the island. Some, such as Labrador tea, blue flag iris and trailing arbutus, are quite common, both on the island and in other parts of Canada. One of the most interesting of these is the pitcher plant, Newfoundland's floral emblem, which grows in peat bogs and feeds mainly on insects it traps in its trumpet-shaped leaves. Other plants, including some orchids, are fairly rare, and still others are very rare. The arctic fleabane, for instance, is known to grow in one place on the island's Humber River and in only three other places in Canada. A variety of mosses grow in boglands as do several kinds of wild berries.

Wildlife
While the forests of Newfoundland abound with wildlife, only about half the species found on the Canadian mainland are native to the island. Among the missing are striped skunks, raccoons and

Left: A few of the 5500 or so woodland caribou that range the Avalon Wilderness Reserve. *Right:* The Cape St. Mary's gannet colony is the largest in Newfoundland and the second largest in North America.

porcupines. Snowshoe hares and chipmunks have been introduced, and so has the now-flourishing moose, brought to the island as a potential food source. Wolves, numerous at one time, have been exterminated. The largest indigenous mammals are the caribou and the black bear, while small fur-bearers include beaver, lynx and red fox. Several species of seals and whales frequent the coastal waters.

Over 200 species of birds nest in Newfoundland, and the island is famous for its seabird sanctuaries. The largest puffin colony on the east coast of North America is found just south of St. John's in the magnificent Bird Islands. In addition to the puffins, kittiwakes, murres, razorbills, thickbills and herring gulls make their home there. Another sanctuary at Cape St. Mary's on the south coast also harbours huge flocks of seabirds. Funk Island, off the northeast coast, provides nesting grounds for thousands more, including 80 percent of North America's common murres. Sadly, however, this island is probably best known for once being home to a massive colony of the now-extinct great auk.

The island has no native reptiles or amphibians, but a few species of frogs and toads have been introduced and the leatherback turtle visits the east coast in summertime.

Labrador

Labrador, the mainland part of the province, lies 20 kilometres (12 miles) across the Strait of Belle Isle from the tip of Newfoundland's Great Northern Peninsula. It is almost three times the size of the island but is like it in having a roughly triangular shape. On the west and south, Labrador shares a border with the province of Quebec; to its east lie the Atlantic Ocean and the Labrador Sea.

Geography and Topography

Labrador is part of the Canadian Shield, an immense arc of ancient rock that curves like a horseshoe around Hudson Bay, covering much of central and eastern Canada.

The most spectacular scenery in Labrador is provided by the rugged Torngat Mountains, which stretch for 200 kilometres (125 miles) in the far north. Rising abruptly from the seacoast, the jagged peaks of the Torngats reach heights of over 1500 metres (5000 feet). Among them is Mount Caubvick (1652 metres/5420 feet), the highest point in the province and the highest peak east of the Rockies. The long coast is indented by countless bays and inlets, and by deep fiords where the land drops steeply into the sea from heights of up to 900 metres (3000 feet).

The vast interior of Labrador is typical Shield plateau, characterized by large areas of swamp and muskeg, with low mountain ranges and rocky ridges rising here and there above a generally featureless landscape. In the west is an area of younger, sedimentary rock, which contains some of the richest iron-ore deposits in North America.

Lakes and Rivers

Labrador has countless lakes and rivers. In the west in particular, there are so many that from the air there appears to be more water than land.

The largest natural body of water within Labrador is Lake

Melville, which is really a 140-kilometre (87-mile) long extension of Hamilton Inlet. Several major rivers, including the Naskaupi, the Goose and the Churchill, flow into Lake Melville. The Churchill, Labrador's longest river, boasts one of Canada's most impressive waterfalls — some 200 metres (600 feet) wide with a vertical drop of 75 metres (246 feet). The falls are now part of a giant hydroelectric project completed in the 1970s. It was this project that pooled the waters of hundreds of lakes and streams to create what is now the largest body of fresh water in Labrador, the Smallwood Reservoir.

Climate

Labrador is said to have the coldest climate for its latitude of any place in the world. Much of it is snow-covered from September to June, and coastal inlets are usually blocked by ice from December to May. The Labrador Current has a chilling effect on coastal summers and brings frequent fogs. In the interior, summers are hotter but winters are colder, and northern winters are colder yet, with temperatures occasionally dropping to -60°C (-76°F). Perhaps it is as some small compensation for the bitterness of the climate that nature offers Labradorians spectacular displays of aurora borealis (northern lights) and an average of 243 clear nights a year on which to be dazzled by them.

Vegetation and Wildlife

The outer coasts and extreme north of Labrador are virtually treeless. Only tundra vegetation is found in these areas — mosses and lichens, a few bright and brave species of arctic flowers, a few hardy berries, and an occasional dwarf willow or birch. The south and west are generally well forested, especially along the rivers, with black spruce and balsam fir predominating.

Polar bears and sea mammals such as seals and whales visit the Labrador coasts, and the forests are well supplied with fur-bearing animals such as beaver, fox, lynx, hare and otter. Among larger mammals, caribou, once the mainstay of the Native peoples of the area, are still plentiful. In fact, the Labrador caribou herd is one of the largest in the world. It is said that grizzly bears once lived in the Torngat Mountains, but only black bears are found there today.

Far left: The spectacular Torngats of Labrador's far north. *Left:* Polar bear. *Below:* Larch and pines and a carpet of "caribou moss" in central Labrador

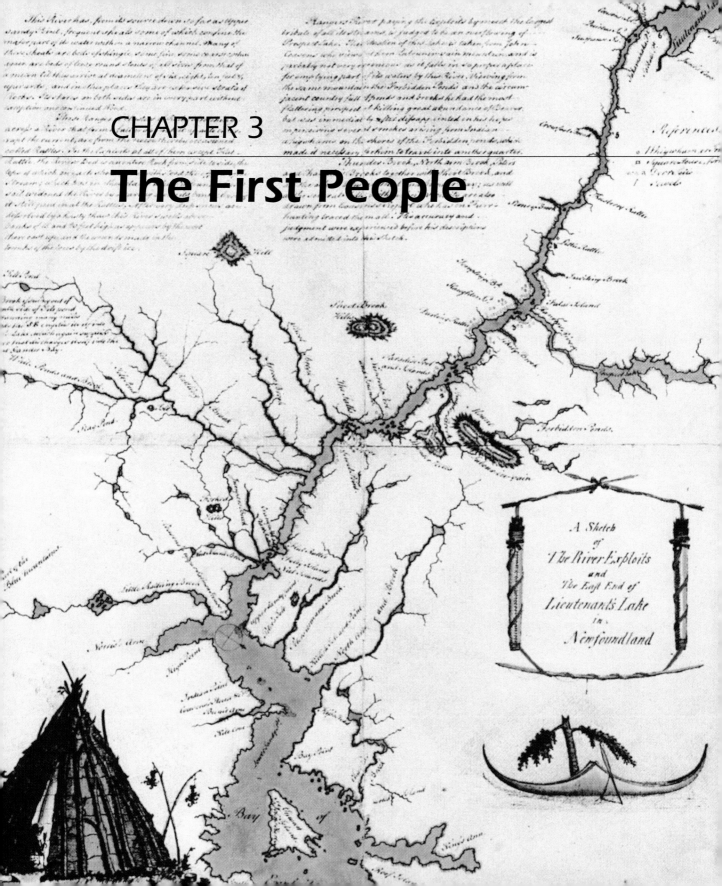

The first people to live in Newfoundland and Labrador reached this part of Canada about 9000 years ago. Much of their long history is still being discovered.

The People of Labrador

The earliest known occupation of Labrador began on the Strait of Belle Isle about 7000 B.C. People we call the Maritime Archaic Indians followed the retreating glaciers to the area, where they hunted large animals and marine mammals. About 4000 years ago, a different culture, called Paleoeskimo, moved into Labrador from the Arctic, displacing the earlier inhabitants. However, about 500 B.C., these people were displaced in their turn by a culture known as the Dorset Eskimo. For a thousand years, the Dorset lived on the land, but they too disappeared, replaced by ancestors of today's Innu and Inuit Labradorians.

The Innu
There are two groups of Innu in Labrador: the Montagnais and the Naskapi. Both belong to the large Algonkian-speaking family of peoples who were spread across the woodlands of central and eastern Canada. The Montagnais lived in the densely forested interior of southern Labrador, the Naskapi to the north of them.

Like other Algonkians, both Montagnais and Naskapi lived primarily by hunting. They therefore moved in regular seasonal

The drawings on John Cartwright's 1768 map of the Exploits River show a Beothuk summer dwelling and the distinctive Beothuk canoe.

Two Naskapi Innu, sketched by William Hind. Because of their remote location in the northern interior, the Naskapi remained relatively unaffected by European settlement longer than most Native groups.

patterns, following the wildlife on which they depended. According to their location and the time of year, they hunted walrus and seal, caribou, bear, beaver and wild birds, using the traditional bow and arrow and bone-headed spears. Fish, berries and roots, caught and gathered in summer, added variety to their diets. Wild plants were also used for healing.

The Innu believed that all things in nature — animals, plants, rivers, rocks — had spirits and that these spirits were very powerful. Animal spirits were especially powerful, and it was very important to seek their favour before a hunt with ceremonies that included songs, dances and drumming. Times of trouble might require the aid of a particularly skilled elder who would communicate with the spirits in a special shaking-tent ceremony.

Inuit hunter poised to throw a bird harpoon from his kayak. The harpoon skimmed along the water and impaled any floating bird in its path.

The Inuit

The Inuit who live in the most northerly part of Labrador are direct descendants of the Thule people who spread eastward from Alaska between A.D. 1000 and 1400. They share their language, Inuktitut, and much of their culture with the other groups of Inuit who live across the Canadian Arctic.

Like other Native groups, Labrador Inuit adapted to the natural resources available to them. In late June, when the last ice disappeared from inshore waters, they moved inland to their summer camping grounds. There they lived on caribou and wild berries. In autumn they moved back to the coast where they hunted seal, fished for salmon and cod, and harpooned Greenland whales from their kayaks. In winter they hunted walrus, polar bears and puffins.

For homes, they made frames of whalebone, which they covered with sod and skins. To light their way at night, they made carved soapstone bowls in which a wick floated in seal oil. Women made clothing from caribou skin, using caribou sinews for thread and needles carved from caribou antlers. They also used sealskin to make winter boots and the covering for hunting kayaks and the larger umiak, in which the family could travel long distances. As well, the women made toys for their children from bone, ivory and strips of leftover animal skins. The men did the hunting, and if they had to be away for several days they built igloos of blocks of ice as temporary shelters. Seal hunting required extraordinary skill and patience. The hunter made a circular hole in the ice and lowered an ivory hook attached to a string into the water. Then he waited, perhaps for hours, completely still but always alert so that when a seal moved the hook, he could instantly spear it with his harpoon.

Island People — The Beothuk

Archaeologists have found that the Maritime Archaic Indians settled the coasts of the island as early as 5500 B.C. The number of tools unearthed indicates that they were the most numerous of all Newfoundland's prehistoric people. About 2500 years ago, the Dorset arrived on the island, but disappeared for reasons that remain unknown. Their successors were the Beothuk.

The Beothuk, who probably came to the island around A.D. 500, are the only Native people whose history belongs exclusively to Newfoundland. Today, there are no Beothuk left. For over a century they were almost forgotten, but their culture is now being rediscovered. Artifacts found at 53 Beothuk burial sites — almost all located in coastal caves or rock shelters along bays and inlets — and the drawings of Shanawdithit, the last known Beothuk, have greatly contributed to our knowledge of their tragic history.

Two of the most important archaeological sites have been found at Port au Choix on the Great Northern Peninsula and at Notre

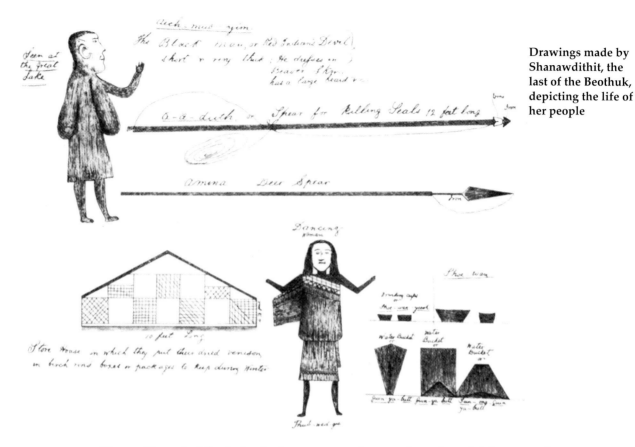

Dame Bay. Artifacts include spear and arrowheads, which were the most common hunting tools. Other objects, such as bone pendants, were preserved with a mixture of red ochre and animal oil. In many cultures red ochre is a symbol of a life-continuing force.

Way of Life

Archaeological evidence indicates that the Beothuk were part of the Algonkian culture and language family. They were creative and adventurous people who knew how to adapt to a demanding climate and terrain.

The Beothuk were clever hunters. They knew the island well and knew where to find cherts, or special stones, to make hunting tools. They built fences that are reported to have stretched up to 48 kilometres (30 miles) along river banks, forcing caribou and deer to cross at a particular place where they could be more easily speared. The Beothuk also knew the habits of animals and the mood of the sea, and knew when to fish and when to hunt and when to gather eggs from seabirds.

During the spring and summer, the Beothuk lived on the coast, where they ate a variety of fish, shellfish and marine mammals. They also smoked meat to preserve it and took advantage of the many berries that grew on the land. In the fall they moved inland, taking shelter in the valley of the Exploits River. There, they followed the migrating caribou herds, travelling in bark canoes until the rivers froze, then on snowshoes made of wooden frames with skin strips. In the early spring they headed back to the coast to hunt seals on the offshore ice. Sometimes the caribou disappeared or changed their migratory pattern, and sometimes harsh winds prevented access to seals off the coast. This led to great hardship and even starvation for some of the Beothuk.

The Beothuk lived in tent-like shelters called *mamateeks* constructed from deerskin or birch bark placed over long poles. In the centre of the mamateek was a fireplace that provided cooking facilities and warmth during the long winter months. Beds made of boughs were set out around the edges. In winter, soil was banked against the outside of the mamateek to keep out the raging elements. A mamateek probably housed between 12 and 15 people. One excavation at Red Indian Lake has revealed a large six-sided mamateek measuring 7.5 by 6 metres (25 by 20 feet).

Most of the time, the Beothuk lived in bands of 35 to 40 people. They had no chiefs, but some individuals had more influence than others. Such people might earn their position by being great hunters. At certain times of the year a number of bands met, often at an interior caribou site. During these meetings, important decisions were made for the upcoming season, and tools, canoes, furs and beads were traded.

Like other Native peoples, the Beothuk believed in a spirit world, and their beliefs influenced all aspects of their daily life. They had great respect for the spirit of the animals they hunted and held special religious feasts, called *mokoshan,* to honour the spirit of the caribou. A large oval structure with two entrances, called a *shaputuan,* was used for these feasts, during which the bones of a caribou were ground up and boiled and the grease skimmed off and eaten.

The Micmac on Tak'am'kuk Island

The Micmac have been a significant presence on the island of Tak'am'kuk, as they call Newfoundland. Like other Native groups, the Micmac have their own system of government, their own religion, customs, values and laws. A Micmac oral tradition, passed from one generation to another, tells of a people who have been here from time immemorial. Proof of their sea voyages can be traced to 1601 when Micmac ancestors came to Newfoundland from Cape Breton to hunt and fish, using small European sailing vessels called *shallops.* There is no evidence to support an old belief that the Micmac were brought to the island by the French and paid to kill the Beothuk. However, the two groups probably did have contact through trade and warfare. By the eighteenth century (and possibly earlier), the Micmac had begun to settle on the island.

Micmac wigwam at St. George's Bay in the early nineteenth century

CHAPTER 4

Europeans
Drop Anchor

Legend tells of St. Brendan, who sailed from Ireland in a leather boat and arrived in Newfoundland around A.D. 500. No proof of the Irish monk's voyage has ever been found, and it seems likely that Europeans did not reach these shores until much later.

The Vikings

More than a thousand years ago Norsemen from the part of Europe we now call Scandinavia sailed their dragon-prowed ships across the Atlantic to explore new lands. Fearless sailors, they became known as Vikings, from a Norse word meaning "camp." They told of their travels in stories called *sagas,* some of which recount their experiences on the shores of Newfoundland and Labrador.

Vikings reached and settled in Greenland about A.D. 982. A few years later, Leif Ericsson, or Leif the Lucky as he was called, heard of other lands to the southwest and set out to explore them. He sailed from Greenland in two *knorrs* — wide, roundish sea-going ships with fixed masts and permanent decks. Eventually Leif came upon a forested coastline with white sandy beaches and with salmon bigger and more plentiful than anyone of his crew had ever seen. This was almost certainly Labrador, which Leif named Markland (meaning woodland). His final stop may have been along Newfoundland's shores, at a place he called Vinland, where the crew fished and repaired their ships. When they returned to Greenland their tales encouraged other expeditions.

Several years later Thorfinn Karlsefni braved the wild seas in his

The town and harbour of St. John's, early 1800s

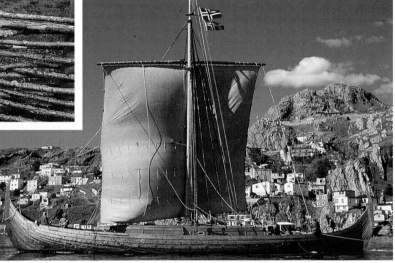

Above: Reconstructed Viking houses at L'Anse aux Meadows, which was declared a World Heritage Site by the United Nations in 1978. *Right:* Replica of a Viking ship

long ships with some 160 would-be settlers. When they landed, they built houses of sod and rock. Gudrid, Thorfinn's wife, gave birth to a son she named Snorri. He was the first European child born in North America and remained here until he was three years old.

The Norse encountered the original inhabitants of Newfoundland and Labrador during their travels. Disputes arose, especially when they tried to establish a settlement. Fights with the Native people, whom they called *skraelings,* as well as the harsh climate and the dangerous seas eventually led them to return to their homeland.

There was no proof of Norse settlements in Newfoundland until 1961, when Norwegian explorer Helge Ingstad and archaeologist Anne Stine Ingstad found the remains of seven Viking dwellings at L'Anse aux Meadows on the Great Northern Peninsula. This remains the only confirmed Viking site in North America, but many people believe that the Vikings explored other areas of the island and perhaps even established settlements elsewhere. The future may therefore bring further interesting discoveries.

European Contact and Exploration

In 1497, an Italian seaman, John Cabot, set sail from Bristol, England, in a small ship called the *Matthew*. After a voyage of 53 days, he dropped anchor, probably in Newfoundland waters near Cape Bonavista, on the northeast coast of the island. It was June 24, St. John's Day in Europe. This day is still commemorated each year with festivities in St. John's, the island's capital city.

Cabot and other explorers of the day braved the high seas in search of a short route to India and the Far East. This was not India, however, and there was no shortcut. But they did find fish. Cabot said that the fish in Newfoundland waters were so plentiful that his crew could simply lower baskets over the side of the ship and pull them up full.

Some historians believe that even before Cabot's voyage, adventurous fisherfolk from Europe had crossed the Atlantic to fish these rich waters. The Basques, people who lived in the hill country between France and Spain, may have already been hunting whales off Newfoundland. Be that as it may, the next known visitor to Newfoundland was a Portuguese explorer named Gaspar Corte-Real, who made a detailed survey of parts of the island's east coast in 1500. Thirty-five years later, French explorer Jacques Cartier used St. John's harbour as a stopping place and proved that Newfoundland was an island by sailing through the Strait of Belle Isle.

The Newfoundland Fishery

Fish was an important product in Europe. Saltfish was in great demand, especially in Catholic countries, where church law decreed that meat should not be eaten on certain days. It is not surprising, therefore, that the rich fishing banks off Newfoundland attracted fisherfolk from many countries — France, Spain, Portugal, England — throughout the sixteenth century. As the fishery expanded, processing of fish on shore became more common. This led to the building of large fish-drying platforms called *flakes*.

As time went on, the Spanish, Portuguese and Basques withdrew from the area, leaving England and France to compete for control of Newfoundland waters. The English operated mainly between Bonavista and Trepassey, along what became known as the English Shore; the French established claims to the "Petit Nord," north of Bonavista, and to the south shore in the Burin and Fortune Bay region. The natural harbour of St. John's proved to be a vital meeting area for sea captains before they spread out along the coastline for months of fishing at a time. At the peak of the fishing industry in the seventeenth century, sailors could walk across the harbour on the decks of the docked ships.

One of the most touching stories to come down to us of these early days is that of Marguerite de Roberval. In 1542, Jean François de la Rocque, Sieur de Roberval, set out to establish a colony on the St. Lawrence River. With him came Marguerite, his niece, and the man he wanted her to marry. Much to his dismay, Marguerite fell in love with one of his sailors. Furious, Roberval put his niece and her nurse, Damienne, ashore on an island, possibly the one now known as Fogo Island, off the coast of Newfoundland. Her lover jumped ship to join her but died a few months later, shortly before Marguerite gave birth to their child. The baby died within a few weeks, as did Damienne. Marguerite survived all alone for over a year and was rescued by a passing French vessel that saw smoke from her fire. She returned to France and worked as a school mistress for many years.

From Fishery to Colony

Throughout the seventeenth and eighteenth centuries, English fisherfolk built temporary and semi-permanent settlements on the island. Most people in these small communities were involved in the fishery. They built shelters for cooking and sleeping, fishing stages to dry the fish and workrooms. To protect their cook houses and fishing nets, some people began to stay on the island year-round. These first settlers cut timber for furniture and boats, and cleared land for vegetable gardens. Thirty-seven years before the Pilgrims landed at Plymouth Rock to become the first English settlers in the present-day United States, sea captains reported their surprise at finding beautiful summer gardens in St. John's.

Basically, however, England and France viewed Newfoundland more as a place to fish than as a colony for permanent settlement, and so the population of the island grew slowly. People shifted back and forth, staying for a few seasons or winters and then returning to Europe. Nonetheless, there were some early attempts to create an English colony on the island that would balance one the French had started on the Bay of Fundy. On May 10, 1610, Bristol merchant John Guy arrived with 41 people to create a settlement on the land now called Cupids. The settlers built houses and a tall stockade with three large guns for protection.

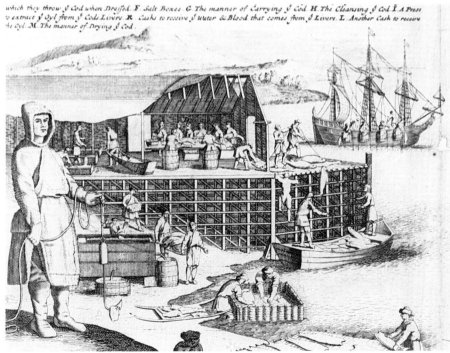

which they throw ỹ Cod when Dressed. F. Salt Boxes. G. The manner of Carrying ỹ Cod. H. The Cleansing ỹ Cod. I. A Press to extract ỹ Oyl from ỹ Cods Livers. R. Casks to receive ỹ water & Blood that comes from ỹ Livers. L. Another Cask to receive the Oyl. M. The manner of Drying ỹ Cod.

View of a fishing stage, showing the steps involved in the "dry" method of curing fish. This lengthy process required a lot of hard work but relatively little salt. It was therefore favoured by the English as salt was scarce and expensive in England. Countries that had access to cheap salt could operate a "wet" or "green" fishery, in which the fish were cleaned and preserved in a lot of salt on the ship.

For various reasons neither this settlement nor any of the others that were attempted lasted very long. Many of the people who came to fish lacked the pioneering skills needed to make a life in this harsh land, and their leaders often wanted a more adventurous life and moved on. Moreover, it was trade that mattered to the merchants in the west of England who sent 200 or 300 ships each year to the Newfoundland fishing grounds. Some worried that permanent settlements might harm their profits, and so they tried to discourage colonization. As if all this were not enough, settlers had to deal with pirates, who found Newfoundland harbours ideal places to hide and refit their ships.

In the early 1600s, pirates were a constant threat to those who sailed on the sea and those who settled on the land. More than once they attacked Cupids, helping themselves to whatever they wanted and carrying off fishermen to serve on their ships.

One of the boldest of these pirates was Peter Easton, who had once been a loyal sailor for the English queen, Elizabeth I. After he turned to piracy, he looted ships in the English Channel, then crossed the Atlantic and set up a fort at Harbour Grace. From there he attacked fishing boats and Spanish and Basque ships, and even raided Puerto Rico in the Caribbean. He has become a folk legend and the subject of many tales, one of which involved his capture of an Irish princess, Sheila Na Geira. It is said that one of Easton's men, Gilbert Pike, jumped ship to help her escape and that they spent the rest of their lives in Carbonear. When Easton finally grew tired of pirating, he bought a palace in Savoy, in southern France, where he retired and lived in luxury.

The Fishing Admirals

In 1634, the English king, Charles I, tried to establish some order in Newfoundland by making the captain of the first ship to reach a harbour each spring the "fishing admiral." In effect, the fishing admirals were the first governors of the island. They often acted in the interest of the merchants back in England, however, rather than in that of the settlers. They applied English laws inconsistently and were often brutal in making decisions and imposing justice. This made things very difficult for those who wanted to make Newfoundland their home, and many disillusioned settlers left. For a time, Newfoundland again became little more than a place to fish.

French – English Conflict

By the mid-1600s, the French and the English were fighting each other not only over the Newfoundland fishery, but over control of North America. Both saw Newfoundland as the key to the shipping lanes in and out of the St. Lawrence River. In 1662, the French fortified and settled Placentia (which they called Plaisance)

View of Placentia today. Established as Plaisance in 1660, this was France's main base in Newfoundland for over 50 years. The strategic advantages of the site are still obvious: the harbour is large, deep, sheltered from winds and ice-free year-round. It was also easy to defend against enemy ships.

The Signal Hill Tattoo is a reminder that France and England fought their last battle over what is now Canada in Newfoundland in 1762.

on the south coast. For many years it remained the French headquarters in Newfoundland.

During the 1690s, the English attacked Placentia several times. In November 1696, the French responded with a major attack on English settlements. Led by Pierre LeMoyne d'Iberville, a party of French soldiers and Micmacs raided Ferryland and other outposts, then walked to St. John's. There they burned virtually everything, packed the inhabitants off to Britain, and then proceeded to destroy the settlements along Conception and Trinity bays. Only at Carbonear Island did the English hold out. The French made no effort to hold the territory, however, and in spring the English colonists returned to St. John's and rebuilt their homes. Within a few months all the settlements had been rebuilt.

In 1708, the French again took St. John's and raids back and forth continued until Britain and France signed a peace treaty in 1713. Under the terms of the treaty, Newfoundland belonged to Britain; the French had to leave Placentia but retained the right to fish and dry their catch along the shore from Cape Bonavista to Pointe Riche. This stretch of coast became known as the French Shore.

Fifty years later, in 1763, France and Britain signed another treaty to end another war, known as the Seven Years' War. All of Canada, including Newfoundland and Labrador, now became British. France received the islands of St. Pierre and Miquelon as a shelter for fishermen, and to this day these islands belong to France. The French were still permitted to fish in Bonavista Bay and Notre Dame Bay, but now Newfoundlanders could also fish there. Over the next 140 years or so, there were ongoing disputes regarding the Newfoundland and French fishing rights. In 1783, the boundaries for the French Shore were changed to extend from Cape St. John on Notre Dame Bay to Cape Ray. Today one area along the French Shore, on the Port au Port Peninsula, is re-establishing its French culture.

European Settlement and the Beothuk

It is estimated that about 2000 Beothuk lived on the island when European fishing fleets began to come regularly to Newfoundland bays. There seems to have been some trading between the Natives and the newcomers during the 1500s, but in general, the Beothuk avoided direct contact with the Europeans and moved away from bays where the fishing boats tended to concentrate.

As European fishing stations multiplied and early settlement developed, however, contact became inevitable. Around 1610, an English merchant, John Guy, met some Beothuk in Trinity Bay and succeeded in making friends with them. When Guy left he promised to come back and trade the following spring.

Accordingly, the Beothuk awaited his return, and when they sighted a ship the next spring, they gathered on the shore. Unfortunately, it was not John Guy's and the captain thought that the Beothuk planned to attack. The English fired shots and the Beothuk, thinking they had been tricked, fought back. This marked the beginning of many such confrontations between the Native people and the English. It was an unequal struggle. Beothuk bows and arrows were no match for the Europeans' guns.

Over the next century and a half, pressure on the Beothuk increased. In time, fishing stations occupied almost every hospitable bay all summer, and more and more Europeans began staying year-round. To avoid encounters with them, the Beothuk were forced to retreat inland. This cut them off from some of their most important food resources. People weakened from malnutrition, and some died of starvation. Others died from diseases introduced by the Europeans.

Eventually British officials realized the damage that had been done and tried to set things right. In 1768, Sir Hugh Palliser, the naval governor, sent Captain John Cartwright on an expedition up the Exploits River to make contact with the Beothuk. Cartwright found only deserted camps. The Beothuk had continued to move farther inland as they grew more fearful of the settlers. Successive governors issued proclamations forbidding the settlers to harm the Beothuk, but already it was too late. Their population was declining rapidly.

Portrait of Demasduit, who was also known by the English name Mary March. After Demasduit died, her body was placed on the shore of Red Indian Lake. Some years later, an explorer found her buried in the traditional Beothuk way beside her husband and child. The gifts she had brought from the authorities at St. John's were found in the burial with her.

In March 1819, a merchant called John Peyton sought out the Beothuk to recover some goods stolen from his fishing premises. His expedition found a Beothuk camp on Red Indian Lake and captured a woman and child after killing her husband and others in the camp. The child died a few days later and the woman, whose Beothuk name was Demasduit, was taken first to Twillingate then to St. John's. The governor decided to send her back to her people on the Bay of Exploits as a gesture of good will. However, a month of searching failed to find any Beothuk. A second effort was made in late 1819, but by this time Demasduit was sick with tuberculosis. She died on the ship on January 8, 1820.

Shanawdithit's Story

A few years later a hungry and sick Beothuk woman and her two daughters surrendered to William Cull in New Bay, Notre Dame Bay. The mother and one daughter died. The other daughter, Shanawdithit, worked as a servant in the household of John Peyton Jr. for five years.

Meanwhile, an explorer named William Cormack had established a society whose purpose was to save the Beothuk from extinction. To this end he organized two expeditions to search the island for survivors. All he found were deserted campsites and burials.

Realizing after his second search that Shanawdithit was probably the last of her people, Cormack had her brought to St. John's in 1828. The intelligent and talented girl told him all she could about her people and did several drawings of them. By this time, Shanawdithit was showing signs of tuberculosis, the disease that had killed her mother and sister. She died on June 6, 1829. Today an unassuming memorial to Shanawdithit and her people stands near the place where she is buried on the south side of St. John's.

The Beothuk probably have some descendants — over the centuries, some almost certainly intermarried with Innu of the mainland and the island Micmac. However, with the death of Shanawdithit, the Beothuk became extinct as a people.

Europeans in Labrador

The fishery was the focus of early European contacts with Labrador as well as with the island.

Basque Whalers

Five hundred years ago, whale oil was in great demand in Europe, where it was used in lamps and for a variety of other purposes. For centuries many Basque seamen had made a specialty of hunting whales, but sometime in the fifteenth century, whales became scarce in European waters. The Basque whalers had to travel farther in search of them, and by the early 1500s they were coming regularly to the Strait of Belle Isle. By 1540, they had established a great whaling station at Red Bay on the Labrador coast.

When the Red Bay whale fishery was at its peak, there might be as many as 20 large ships in the port and 2000 people involved in working at sea or on shore. The whalers harpooned the huge mammals from small boats. Onshore workers cut the fat from the whales, boiled it in huge cauldrons to extract the oil, poured the oil into barrels and loaded it on the ships.

The Basque whalers operated in Red Bay for over a hundred years, but eventually the whales became rare here too and the whaling station was abandoned.

Settlers in Labrador

Settlement along the coast of southern Labrador followed much the same pattern as on the island, but it proceeded even more slowly. In the 1500s and 1600s, ships from Europe anchored in Labrador bays for the summer. Some dried their fish on shore; all headed back to Europe in the fall.

In time, as settlement increased on the island, Newfoundlanders too began to come to fish in Labrador bays, and a few, known as *livyers*, began to stay on through the winter. Those who just spent the summer ashore were called *stationers*, and those who took their

Excavations at Red Bay. Archaeological teams that work here every summer have unearthed many tools and other items dating back to the Basque whaling station.

catch back to their home port without coming ashore at all were called *floaters*. Labrador was an even harsher land than the island, so those who decided to make it their home were never numerous. Still, a few people did set up businesses, and a few small but permanent settlements were established in sheltered bays.

Settlement and the Native Peoples

Unlike the Beothuk of the island, the Innu of southern Labrador quite quickly established friendly relations with the Europeans. They seem to have traded early on with fishing crews that came ashore, and later they became an important part of New France's fur trade network.

In time, they came to depend on European trade items such as metal goods, cloth and firearms. When the St. Lawrence fur trade all but died out in the 1820s, this dependence caused the Innu great hardship. To make matters worse, farmers and loggers began encroaching on their hunting grounds.

Many Innu still organize a two- or three-month hunting trip into the interior every year, flying to and from their camping place by small chartered aircraft. Seen here in their bush camp are a woman cutting boughs for the floor of the family tent and a baby safely and snugly installed in a *nenepishum,* a kind of hammock that many Innu set up in their village homes as well.

Fortunately, the Innu had the freedom of the vast, animal-rich interior, which was too remote to be of much interest to non-Natives. They withdrew farther inland where they were able, for a time, to maintain their traditional hunting and fishing way of life.

Like the Innu, the Inuit were eager for European goods, but they mistrusted the newcomers. And not without reason: several early explorers and sea captains had carried Inuit captives off to Europe to display as curiosities or use as slaves. Nonetheless, the Inuit did establish trade relations with fishing crews, but they fiercely opposed settlement and any effort to limit their access to bays and inlets where they hunted and fished.

By 1763, when Sir Hugh Palliser became governor of Newfoundland, a state of almost constant warfare existed between Inuit and whites. A year or two later Jens Haven, a member of a missionary group called the Moravian Brethren, wanted to

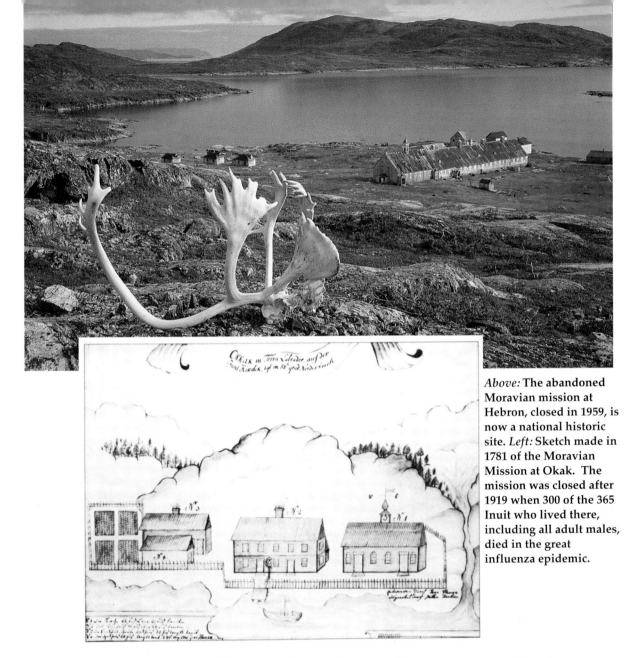

Above: The abandoned Moravian mission at Hebron, closed in 1959, is now a national historic site. *Left:* Sketch made in 1781 of the Moravian Mission at Okak. The mission was closed after 1919 when 300 of the 365 Inuit who lived there, including all adult males, died in the great influenza epidemic.

establish a mission for the Labrador Inuit. Palliser encouraged him in the hope that he might be able to do something to end the fighting.

Haven had learned Inuktitut in Greenland, and his ability to communicate with the Inuit enabled him to set up missions in Nain and later in Hopedale, Makkovik and Okak. Peace was restored along the coast, and a close relationship developed between the Inuit and the Moravians that would last well into the twentieth century.

CHAPTER 5

Colony and Dominion

When England and France finally ended their last war over North America in 1763, the population of Newfoundland was barely 10 000. Thirty years later, it had tripled, and 30 years after that it had reached 60 000.

Britain's involvement in other wars — the American War of Independence (1775-1783) and, especially, the Napoleonic wars (1793-1815) — had a lot to do with the increase. It became both too costly and too dangerous to operate the Newfoundland fishery from English bases. At the same time, war increased the demand for Newfoundland fish and raised the price. The result was a dramatic growth of the resident fishery. Outport communities sprang up by the dozens; St. John's grew by leaps and bounds as the supply centre for the outports and the marketing centre for the catch. The expanding economy attracted merchants and professionals as well as large numbers of Britain's poor — Irish, Scottish and English — in search of work and a better life. The 1830s and 1840s saw another surge in population as thousands of the million or so Irish who were driven out of their country by terrible famines settled in Newfoundland.

Political Evolution

In spite of the increase in population, the British government took a long time to get over the idea that Newfoundland was just a place to fish. Through to 1817, the naval governors regularly returned to England for the winter, leaving behind only a haphazard and arbitrary system for enforcing the law and administering justice. And

Downtown St. John's in the 1850s

The Colonial Building, seat of the Newfoundland legislature 1850-1934 and 1949-59. *Insets:* William Carson (left) and Patrick Morris, allies in the struggle for representative government. Both served in the House of Assembly after their goal was achieved.

not until 1824 did Britain finally recognize Newfoundland as a colony and provide for a civil governor and council. By this time, however, Newfoundlanders were beginning to demand more than a stable, island-based government. They wanted some real control over their own affairs. Among those calling for reform were Dr. William Carson and Patrick Morris.

Carson, a doctor, came to Newfoundland from Scotland in 1808. Almost immediately he began to call for improvements in the health, agriculture and government of the colony. He helped found the first hospital in St. John's, and with Morris, a merchant and farmer who had come from Ireland as a child, he helped people get title to their land. Morris encouraged clearing land to grow crops so that there was less need to bring in food from outside. He also helped establish a school and an orphanage for the poor.

Thanks largely to the tireless effort of these two men, Newfoundlanders were given representative government in 1832: they could now elect local people to an Assembly, to help the governor run the colony. The governor was appointed by Britain, however, and he chose his own council of advisors. While the Assembly voted on laws, the governor and his council did not have to abide by its wishes.

During the 1840s, people in other British North American colonies were demanding a government that was answerable to their elected representatives. This is known as responsible government, and Nova Scotia was the first to achieve it in 1848. It took a little longer for reformers in Newfoundland to overcome local opposition and the resistance of British politicians. Finally, in 1855, the governor of Newfoundland was instructed to appoint his Executive Council from members of the elected Legislative Assembly. The English governor still had to sign laws passed by the legislature and retained some other limited powers.

On Its Own

In the 1860s, the British North American colonies discussed the idea of getting together to form a single country. The Dominion of Canada was created in 1867 when the colonies of Nova Scotia, New Brunswick and the United Province of Canada joined in Confederation. Newfoundland had sent representatives to a conference held to work out the terms of union, but did not hold a vote on the subject until 1869. Supporters of Confederation argued that joining would bring many economic benefits; opponents argued that it would more likely bring new taxes. As it happened, the fishery was having its first good year of the decade, and Newfoundlanders decided to continue on their independent way.

The rest of the nineteenth century and the early years of the twentieth brought many changes to Newfoundland and Labrador. St. John's continued to develop as a lively commercial and administrative centre. It got its first electric lights, powered by steam-driven generators, in 1885; fifteen years later its first street railway was running on electricity produced by the island's first hydro power station at nearby Petty Harbour. In between, in 1892,

Old St. John's after the fire that destroyed half of the city in 1892

much of the city had to be rebuilt after a devastating fire that left 11 000 people homeless.

Beyond the capital, settlement continued to spread as the outport fishery expanded and as attempts to diversify the economy bore fruit. Copper discoveries in the 1850s led the government to sponsor a geological survey of the island's resources. Construction of a trans-island railway began in 1881, and the first scheduled ferry service went into operation between Port aux Basques and Cape Breton Island in 1897. The coast of the Great Northern Peninsula became available for settlement in 1904 when French fishing rights were revoked. Five years later, the first pulp and paper mill was established at Grand Falls, creating off-season jobs for fishermen and giving the island what has been called its "first community out of sight and sound of the sea."

This period saw the first efforts to improve the quality of life in remote communities. In 1892, Wilfred Grenfell, an English medical missionary, visited the Labrador coast for the first time and was appalled by the poverty and lack of medical care he found in the fishing communities. He opened his first hospital at Battle Harbour the following year. Other hospitals, nursing stations and orphanages followed as Grenfell devoted the rest of his life to the welfare of the people of Labrador and northern Newfoundland. On a different front, William Ford Coaker organized the Fishermen's

Labrador fishing family and their sod house in the 1890s. *Inset:* Monument to Dr. Wilfred Grenfell at St. Anthony, headquarters of the Grenfell Mission. In addition to organizing medical and other social services for the remote communities of Newfoundland and Labrador, Grenfell established co-operatives, recruited supporters and raised the funds to keep his work going.

Protective Union in 1908 to improve conditions not just for fishermen but for other working people as well.

One of the most remarkable self-help organizations was the Newfoundland Organization of Nurses Industrial Association (NONIA), established in the 1920s to bring nursing services to outports that had no resident doctor or nurse. NONIA nurses worked extremely hard for very little pay. Communites wishing to become a part of NONIA formed local committees making hand-knitted goods as a way of helping pay for the service. Sale of these goods covered 75 percent of the nurses' salaries; the government paid the rest. The nursing side of NONIA ended in 1934 when the Commission Government assumed responsibility for health care in the outports. The organization survived, however, as a way for outport women to bridge their isolation and contribute to the local economy.

The Great War

During the First World War (1914-18) Newfoundland contributed many men to the British navy and raised its own army regiment. Newfoundland women served overseas as nurses and ambulance drivers. By the war's end, more than 4000 Newfoundlanders had been killed or wounded overseas. Today, each July 1, the people of Newfoundland and Labrador join other Canadians in celebrating

Canada Day, but they also take time to mourn the hundreds of Newfoundlanders who gave their lives on July 1, 1916, in the Battle of Beaumont Hamel in France.

Labrador also suffered from the war, but in a different way. The Spanish flu, brought back in 1918 by returning soldiers, killed 50 000 Canadians. It hit coastal Labrador especially hard. A mission ship, *Harmony*, carrying annual supplies to Hopedale and Nain had a crew member who was sick with influenza. As the villagers mixed with the crew, they were infected, and the disease spread rapidly. Whole communities, many of them Inuit, were wiped out.

One of the many stories about the tragedy was told by Martha Joshua, a young Inuit girl who was travelling with her family to their traditional hunting grounds when the Spanish flu struck. On a tiny island near Okak, all the others died leaving her alone with the husky dogs. She lived on snow and hard bread for three months until some hunters found her.

Labrador's Uncertain Owners

Until the end of the Seven Years' War in 1763, southern Labrador, including Hamilton Inlet, was considered to be part of New France. Then it became part of Britain's North American colonies, with no exact boundary. When the British government appointed a governor for Newfoundland, he was made responsible for the "coast" of Labrador.

Labrador was transferred to the colony of Quebec by the Quebec Act of 1774, but in 1809 it was given back to Newfoundland. In 1825, the British government set the southern boundary between Quebec and Labrador at a line going north from the harbour of Blanc Sablon and then west along the 52nd parallel. The rest of the interior boundary, however, was not defined. Finally, in 1927, a British court accepted Newfoundland's claim to the watershed of all the rivers that flow into the Atlantic and set the western boundary that exists today.

The Women's Suffrage Movement

Even after self-government was achieved, a large segment of the population continued to have no say in how they were governed. Women were directly affected by the laws of the land, but their struggle to gain the right to vote continued for more than 50 years. The Women's Suffrage Movement began in the late 1880s, led by members of the Women's Christian Temperance Union. An influential organization within the Methodist Church, the WCTU worked with the homeless and unemployed. Its members were convinced that alcohol added greatly to social problems and that women needed the vote if things were to improve.

With the outbreak of the First World War in 1914, the suffrage movement took a back seat to the crisis at hand. But the Women's Patriotic Association, initially set up to make knitted supplies for the men overseas, served to unite women scattered across the province. When the war ended, women resumed their struggle for the vote with renewed vigour under stalwart leaders like Fannie McNeil, May Kennedy and Julia Salter Earle. Finally, in 1925 Sir Richard Squires, their main opponent, resigned as prime minister and his successor, Walter S. Monroe, introduced and passed the Women's Suffrage Bill.

McNeil, Kennedy and Earle ran in the next municipal election, but were unsuccessful. Earle lost by a narrow margin. Several years later, a man on his death bed confessed that he had removed enough ballots from a voters' box to defeat her. This is but one example of the enormous obstacles women faced when they tried to run for public office. In 1928, Helena Squires, wife of Sir Richard, became the first woman to hold public office. However, it would be over 40 years before another woman, Hazel MacIsaac, was elected. She was followed by Hazel Newhook and Lynn Verge in 1979. By 1993, women were mayors of two of Newfoundland's largest cities, but they continued to be under-represented in federal and provincial politics.

Setbacks and Commission Government

After the war, there was a brief period of prosperity. But Newfoundland was burdened with a huge debt caused by the war and the cost of building the railway. Then came the worldwide depression of the 1930s. Markets for Newfoundland products collapsed and tax revenues plummeted as thousands of people were thrown out of work. By 1933, the government was so desperate for money that it tried to sell Labrador to Canada for $10 million. Canada couldn't afford the price.

Finally, unable to pay the interest on its debt or provide the services its people needed, the government turned to Britain for help. In 1934, Commission Government was set up, ending Newfoundland's self-government and returning the island to colonial status. Newfoundland was now administered by an appointed British governor and an appointed commission of six men, three from Britain and three from Newfoundland. While Commission Government did bring some relief, one in three Newfoundlanders was still living on "the dole," receiving six cents a day in 1938. Commission Government remained in effect until Newfoundland joined the Confederation of Canada in 1949.

Early in 1932, when thousands of Newfoundlanders were unemployed and almost destitute, charges of corruption were brought against government officials, including the prime minister, Sir Richard Squires. On April 5, demonstrators gathered outside the House of Assembly to demand an investigation of the charges. What began as a orderly march turned into a riot. Squires escaped through a side door, but the Colonial Building was badly damaged before the police managed to disperse the mob.

The Second World War

The economic tide turned with the start of the Second World War in 1939. Demand for Newfoundland resources, such as iron ore and fish, rose sharply. More crucially, both for the war effort and the economy, Newfoundland's location made it a vital station on North America's air and sea routes to Europe. Convoys of merchant ships with supplies for Britain met the warships assigned to defend them in St. John's harbour before setting off across the Atlantic. Five new airports were built at St. John's, Torbay, Gander, Stephenville and Goose Bay, as well as two naval and several army bases.

The defence construction boom provided jobs, at good pay, for thousands of Newfoundlanders. At the same time, the island's strategic importance brought the war right to its coasts: German submarines made raids in Conception Bay in 1942, and that same year, the Newfoundland ferry *Caribou* was torpedoed and sunk on its run between Nova Scotia and Port aux Basques. Of the 137 people killed, many were women and children.

There were other tragedies — thousands of Newfoundland's young men and women served in the British and Canadian forces or in the merchant marine, and many lost their lives. At the same time, the war gave many Newfoundlanders their first taste of prosperity, as well as their first encounter with a modern North American lifestyle. They liked it, and the experience would be a factor a few years later when they had to decide on their future.

This Hudson Bomber on display at Gander is a reminder of the airfield's crucial role during the Second World War. At one point, planes manufactured in North America were taking off for Britain at the rate of one a minute.

CHAPTER 6

A Province of Canada

After the war, Britain asked Newfoundlanders to decide what they wanted done about their government. Basically they had three choices: they could stay as they were, governed by a commission; they could go back to being an independent self-governed dominion as they had been before 1934; or they could join Canada.

Many fierce debates took place, particularly between those who favoured independence and those who supported union with Canada. The former, led by Peter Cashin, appealed to Newfoundlanders' independent nature and to their pride in their separate culture and history. The pro-Confederates, led by Joey Smallwood, argued that as part of a larger, richer Canada, Newfoundlanders would benefit from such social programs as unemployment insurance, old age pensions and family allowances, which would protect them from the dire poverty they had always known in bad economic times.

In the end, two votes had to be held before the matter was decided. In the first, independence won the most votes but not a majority. Commission Government, which had won the fewest, was dropped as an option, and this time Confederation won by a narrow margin (78 323 to 71 334). Just before midnight on March 31, 1949, Newfoundland and Labrador became Canada's tenth province.

The Confederation Building, headquarters of the provincial government and meeting place of the House of Assembly. It was built in 1959 to mark the tenth anniversary of Newfoundland's entry in Confederation.

Government and Politics

From the start, Newfoundland has been represented at the federal level by six appointed senators and seven elected members of Parliament. While the number of MP's is small, Newfoundlanders such as Don Jamieson, John Crosbie, James McGrath and Brian Tobin have been leading figures in federal politics.

Provincial Government

Joey Smallwood became the first premier of Newfoundland and Labrador, and his Liberal government shaped the politics of the province for over 20 years. Smallwood was a charismatic leader who became known throughout Canada as defender of the rights of Newfoundlanders. Under his guidance the province made great advances in social welfare and education; however, Smallwood was also involved in a number of controversial decisions.

Foremost among these was the resettlement program undertaken in the mid-1950s. Its object was to move people out of the outports into larger centres where it would be easier and cheaper to provide services for them and, in theory, easier for them to find work. Over 20 years or so, about 40 000 people were uprooted under this program. Some adjusted well to their new life, but for many the move brought mainly homesickness and disappointment. Government plans to attract new industries and jobs to the province did not meet with much success: Newfoundland was too sparsely populated and too far from major North American centres for companies to want to set up factories there.

Another decision for which the Smallwood government would later be much criticized had to do with developing the huge hydroelectric potential of Churchill Falls in Labrador. In order to get this gigantic project underway in the late 1960s, the government agreed to a contract selling most of the power to Hydro-Québec at a set price for the next 65 years. There was no provision in the contract to raise this price to allow for inflation or any other

The Smallwood years (*clockwise from top left:*) Joey Smallwood signs the agreement admitting Newfoundland to Confederation; underground installations at the Churchill Falls hydroelectric station; Corner Brook, Newfoundland's second city was incorporated in 1955; Cape Freels, after resettlement. In time some people drifted back to their old homes, but over 200 outports remain ghost towns.

circumstance, even though Hydro-Québec was free to resell the electricity in the United States for whatever price it could get. As a result, when energy prices skyrocketed in the mid-1970s, it was Quebeckers who reaped the benefits of Labrador's hydro resources, not Newfoundlanders and Labradorians. A later government tried to find a legal way out of the disastrous contract but failed.

In the early 1970s, in spite of improvements in their standard of living, many Newfoundlanders and Labradorians felt that the province was progressing too slowly. They rejected Joey

A Newfoundland success story — the Marystown shipyard. As well as steel draggers, the shipyard has been producing oil-drilling ships equipped with specialized computers and highly sophisticated location equipment.

Smallwood's leadership and for the next 16 years, under Frank Moores and Brian Peckford, a Progressive Conservative government ruled the province. Throughout this time, the province continued to try to improve the economic conditions of the people. Hopes centred on the development of offshore oil, but for several years the government was locked in conflict with Ottawa over ownership and control of that resource. Finally an agreement was reached on the division of oil revenue, but environmental concerns and a drop in oil prices created further delays. During the 1980s, the Canadian economy went into recession, and Newfoundland and Labrador suffered longer and more than most. Strikes and back-to-work legislation made the government unpopular, and in 1989, the Liberals, now led by Clyde Wells, returned to office. Premier Wells was re-elected on May 3, 1993, with 36 seats. The Progressive Conservatives were left with 15 seats and the New Democratic Party, led by Jack Harris, took one seat.

Municipal Government

Conventional local government was slow to develop in Newfoundland. St. John's elected its first council in 1888, and at Confederation in 1949, there were only some 20 municipal governments. Municipal governments provide a wide variety of services, such as roads, sewers, waste management, water supply, police and fire protection, libraries, and in the larger communities, public transportation. Today there are three incorporated cities: St. John's, Mount Pearl, and Corner Brook. As well, there are at least 170 communities administered as towns. More than 300 smaller communities have no local government at all.

Influences In Education

Religion in Newfoundland and Labrador has always gone hand in hand with education. The earliest schools were established in the first half of the eighteenth century by an Anglican missionary group called the Society for the Propagation of the Gospel in Foreign Parts. By the end of the century, Irish Catholics and some Methodists who were preaching in Conception Bay had also set up a few schools. One result of the religious nature of the schools was that one place might have several, if several churches were active there, while many places had no school at all. Government first began to take some responsibility for education in 1836, but it was not until the Education Act of 1920 that the Department of Education was established and a school curriculum developed.

Right up until Confederation in 1949, education was largely carried out in one-room schools and most students stayed only until grade six.

The Education System Today

The province still has a denominational system of education. Under this unique and controversial arrangement, responsibility is shared between the provincial government and Education Councils of the major denominations: integrated (Protestant), Roman Catholic and Pentecostal. The money allocated each year by the government goes to the 27 school boards for operating and maintenance costs. The Denominational Education Councils determine capital expenditures and the type of religious curriculum to be taught. There are also five French-language schools and a growing French immersion program. Today about 35 percent of the province's people are Roman Catholic and about 60 percent belong to the Protestant churches including the Anglican, Moravian, United, Presbyterian, Salvation Army and the Pentecostal Assemblies.

Right: Roman Catholic school at Pouch Cove, 1948. *Far right:* The Arts and Education Building, Memorial University, St. John's

In recent decades, Newfoundland has received a sizeable number of non-Christian immigrants who have brought with them their own spiritual beliefs. Today there are strong Jewish, Bahai and Buddhist communities. Because of this, school boards are beginning to reassess the role of religion in schools. The 1992 Williams Royal Commission Report recommended that co-operation in joint services was essential in the interest of students. In response to the report, government began discussions on restructuring the school system.

Post-Secondary Education
Several modern post-secondary institutions have made a major contribution to the modernization of Newfoundland and Labrador. These include Memorial University, the Fisheries and Marine Institute of Memorial University, Sir Wilfred Grenfell College in Corner Brook and the Colleges of Applied Arts, Technology and Continuing Education. Memorial University, one of the largest universities in Atlantic Canada, is renowned for its Folklore Department, its School of Medicine and its Earth Science programs. The Marine Institute has been a catalyst for economic development in the fishing and marine industries. The Institute of Social and Economic Research was established in 1961 to foster research on the geography and culture of the province.

Technical colleges in the province offer vocational training in many skilled areas, such as print making, carpentry, mechanics, drafting and computer technology. Five regional community colleges with several campuses address adult education needs.

Native People Today

As the Europeans developed and extended their way of life across the length and breadth of Newfoundland and Labrador, the surviving Native peoples of the province faced many challenges.

Through most of the nineteenth century, the island Micmac were

Above: **Innu protest low-level flight training at Goose Bay, 1989. Chief Daniel Ashini addresses the crowd.** *Top right:* **Young Micmac dancers after their performance.** *Right:* **Inuit boys, Nain**

able to live much as their ancestors had, their dealings with the newcomers occurring mainly as they themselves chose. When settlement spread to the interior and the west, change was inevitable. Many took jobs in the lumber camps, learned English, sent their children to school.

Today the Micmac live mostly on the Conne River reserve along the south coast of the island. The 700 people on the reserve are recognized by the federal government as Status Indians. They are re-establishing their culture and use of the Micmac language in their school system, and, like other Native peoples in Canada, are in the process of negotiating land claims.

Change was particularly difficult in Labrador. After the devastation of the Spanish flu, the Inuit population is again increasing, and has reached its highest level ever along the coast. The lifestyle has changed, however. The Inuit now live in frame houses in settled communities at Nain, Hopedale and Makkovik. However, many still spend the summer farther north fishing for arctic char, and they continue to follow many of the old traditions.

For the Labrador Innu, most of whom live along the coast at Davis Inlet and at Sheshatshiu on Lake Melville, the advance of a modern lifestyle has been tragic. Like the outport people in Newfoundland, the Davis Inlet Innu were resettled there by the provincial government. Over the years, they have found it increasingly difficult to maintain their traditional hunting and fishing way of life, and most have become dependent on government assistance. Under the terms of Confederation, the province has responsibility for Native affairs in Labrador, but it does not provide the same level of services and financial support that Native people in the rest of Canada receive. Despite promises, the Davis Inlet community has no running water or sewage system and there is no work. Substance abuse is very high, especially among the young people. The Innu are asking to be relocated to Sango Bay where they hope to re-establish a lifestyle based on their traditional values.

The Innu living in Sheshatshiu near Happy Valley-Goose Bay have also been affected by modern life. When Goose Bay became a major air base during the war, the non-Native population quickly tripled, threatening the Innu's hunting and trapping way of life. After the war things got even worse as iron mines attracted yet more outsiders, vast areas of Innu hunting territory were flooded for the Churchill Falls hydro project, and the use of Goose Bay for NATO flight testing disrupted the wildlife.

Since the 1970s, the Innu have been protesting these developments, and both Innu and Inuit have made claims to land that will be theirs to control. Land rights are more easily defined for the Inuit than for the Innu since the Inuit have been settled in a particular area for some time and have not been pressured by outside settlement. The Innu have been displaced by industry that supports thousands of white settlers who now consider Labrador their home. Neither the federal nor the provincial government really disputes the justice of Native land claims in principle. Agreeing on specifics, however, will not be easy and negotiations are expected to go on for several years.

CHAPTER 7

The Sea

More than anything else, the sea has shaped the history, the way of life and the culture of Newfoundland and Labrador. No matter what changes may lie ahead for the fishing industry, the sea will continue to dominate Newfoundland's existence.

On The Grand Banks

There are several fishing banks off the coast of Newfoundland and Labrador, but the most famous is the Grand Banks. This level underwater plain is almost as big as Newfoundland itself and lies between 100 and 200 metres (50 and 100 fathoms) below the surface of the sea. The cold Labrador Current meets the warm Gulf Stream here, agitating the water and stirring up nutrients from the seafloor. Because of the relative shallowness of the water, sunlight reaches the bottom and fosters the growth of tiny plant and animal organisms called *plankton*. Plankton provides food for many small fish, such as caplin, which in turn are food for cod and other groundfish. Until recently, it was believed that the cod would last forever.

Fishing Rights

For centuries, Newfoundlanders and Canadians have shared the banks fishery with other countries. Until fairly recently, international agreements set the limit of a country's control over its waters at five kilometres (three miles) from shore. Everything

Fishing gear on the dock at Petty Harbour

beyond that (including the Grand Banks) was international waters where any country could fish as much as it wanted.

Since Confederation in 1949, the federal government has had jurisdiction over the fishery, though there is a provincial fishery department as well. For many years, successive provincial governments have called for joint management of the industry because Newfoundland believes that the people who live on and around the sea know what is best for it. Meanwhile, in 1977, Canada's zone of control over fishing grounds was extended to 320 kilometres (200 miles), which meant that Canada could now regulate fishing activity over much of the Grand Banks.

The Fishing Economy

Much of the cod and other species of groundfish caught on the Newfoundland fishing banks and along the Labrador coast has been fished from large offshore vessels. For many years, the famous salt bankers, sailing ships especially built for banks fishing, were the mainstay of the fishery. Ships and crews left their home ports in Newfoundland, Canada, the United States and Europe, and fished the banks for weeks at a time. They returned home loaded with saltfish to sell in distant markets. Later, steam-powered trawlers replaced the salt bankers.

Traditionally, many Newfoundlanders fished the shallow waters around the province. These inshore fisherfolk moved through the coves and inlets and continued the old tradition of using fishing sheds and flakes for salting and drying the fish. In the late nineteenth century, many inshore fisherfolk, especially those from the south shore, began to go farther out to sea in schooners, though they did their actual fishing from *dories* — small, narrow boats with flat bottoms. They thus joined the offshore fishery, staying out on the banks for weeks and salting their catch on board.

Either way, Newfoundlanders then sold their salted fish and other sea products to merchants, who then sold them overseas. At

Left: Women in fishing families often had to shoulder most of the everyday responsibilities for home, children and community affairs. Many also worked the stages, where the fish were split and salted and tended to the fish drying on flakes.
Right: Hauling in nets off Twillingate. At one time it would have been highly unusual to find a woman fishing at sea alongside the men. By the early 1990s, it was fairly common.

the same time, the merchants brought goods into Newfoundland, thus controlling the trade in both directions. Whole communities bought food and supplies on credit or bartered fish in exchange for items they needed — money was seldom a part of the transaction. This system worked until a poor fishing season left whole communities hopelessly in debt to the merchants. In such hard times, people shared what they had to help one another survive.

As the industry changed, so did the work of women in the fishery. Large modern fish processing plants replaced the many small flakes and stages. These new plants hired thousands of Newfoundlanders, mostly women.

Improving a Way of Life

In 1908, William Ford Coaker tried to organize workers in the fishery by founding the Fishermen's Protective Union. Within a few years the union had 20 000 members, mainly in the northeast coast area. Coaker believed the whole community should be involved in the effort to improve conditions for Newfoundland workers. He also believed in political action. In the 1920s, he became fisheries minister in the government, but was unable to bring about real and lasting change in the industry. A collapse in the saltfish market and the economic depression of the 1930s brought the union down.

Mid-Century Developments

After Confederation, technological developments and government money transformed Newfoundland's fishery. Loans enabled individuals to obtain better craft and equipment. Fish companies were able to expand their processing plants and acquire diesel-powered trawlers and draggers capable of gathering huge quantities of fish. Refrigeration units on board eliminated the need for salting. The saltfish industry declined, and the market for fresh-frozen fish increased rapidly. As well, organization of the fishery was revived under Richard Cashin, who established the Fishermen's Union in 1970. By the 1980s, it had become the biggest union in the province.

The Seal Fishery

An annual harvest of seals has always been a part of the Newfoundland fishery. From the earliest times, Native peoples left their inland camps in late winter to be at the coast when ice floes moved down from the Arctic, bringing with them thousands of seals.

In the eighteenth century, harp seals were so plentiful that they could sometimes be caught in nets on ice piled up at the shore. But it was farther out at sea on the drifting floes that the harp mothers gave birth and stayed gathered in huge numbers until the young seals, known as whitecoats, were strong enough to swim to the Arctic. European settlers soon realized that they could catch many more seals by taking boats out among the floes. By the 1850s, 400 vessels carried 10 000 men to the ice each spring and brought back as many as 700 000 seals in a single season.

In the early days, the main value of the seals was the oil that could be produced from their fat. The meat was appreciated and the pelts

Above: The greatest danger for sealers was the possibility of getting carried away from the ship in a storm and being stranded on the drifting ice. *Far left:* Living quarters aboard a sealing ship, 1950. *Left:* Statue of Sir William Coaker, who has been called "the man who taught the fishermen of Newfoundland to take charge of their own destiny"

were used for clothing, but it was the oil that put cash into Newfoundlanders' pockets at a time when the fishing economy was based primarily on an exchange of goods. Later, when the demand for seal oil declined, the pelts of the whitecoats became the main commercial focus of the hunt.

Animal Rights Protest

About 25 years ago animal rights activists and environmental groups mounted a worldwide campaign against the seal hunt.

Protesters even landed on the ice and spray-painted the whitecoats so that their fur would be worthless.

This has been a difficult issue for Newfoundlanders, who believe themselves to be a gentle breed of people. On the whole, many of them found the campaign insulting and unfair. They also believe that the seals harmed the fishery by competing with the cod for food.

The protests succeeded in putting an end to the seal hunt, but there is much debate in Newfoundland about the effect of the resulting increase in the seal population on the fishery. Studies suggest there are humane ways of taking the harp seals, and there is talk about re-opening the hunt. It is clear, however, that it will never again be what it was in the past.

A Heavy Price

The sea exacted a price for the bounty it provided.

No one really knows how many lives were lost in the fogs and storms or in the many kinds of accidents that could befall a fishing vessel in the wild Atlantic waters. And sealing was even more dangerous than fishing because of the shifting ice. Many are the stories of sealing disasters when men risked "death on the ice," in the words of Newfoundland writer Cassie Brown.

Over the years, Newfoundland and Labrador have witnessed more than 700 shipwrecks. A few made headlines around the world. Probably the most famous of the doomed ships was the *Titanic*, which sank in 1912, on its first voyage from England. More recently, there is the haunting memory of the tragic sinking of the oil rig *Ocean Ranger* in 1982, in which more than 80 men lost their lives.

> ### EROSION
>
> It took the sea a thousand years,
> A thousand years to trace
> The granite features of this cliff,
> In crag and scarp and base.
>
> It took the sea an hour one night,
> An hour of storm to place
> The sculpture of these granite seams
> Upon a woman's face.
>
> E.J. Pratt

Crisis In The Fishery

The deep sea fishery provided a living for Newfoundland fisherfolk for centuries. However, over the last decade or two there have been ever more alarming signs of overfishing and declining fish stocks. The large draggers catch every kind and size of fish, leaving fewer and fewer to spawn for the future fishery.

The establishment of the 320-kilometre (200-mile) limit by Canada helped to control foreign fishing within most of Newfoundland's waters. However, overfishing has continued on parts of the Grand Banks outside the 320-kilometre zone, and Canadian draggers inside the zone have wastefully scooped up hundreds of millions of immature fish, contributing to the decline in fish stocks. Unlike sport fishing where undersized fish are returned alive to the stream, the undersized fish caught in this way are long past saving by the time they are sorted and dumped back into the ocean.

Cod Moratorium

In March 1992, the then federal minister of fisheries, John Crosbie, announced a two-year moratorium on the northern cod fishery. The ecosystem of ocean life was at risk. Simply put, the fish stocks were no longer there. The moratorium affected 25 000 fish plant workers,

Fishing in Conception Bay

trawler workers and fisherfolk, who became dependent on the $500-million compensation package offered by the federal government. Newfoundland's unique community-based lifestyle and all related businesses and industries — from family-owned fish and chip take-outs to large trucking companies — have also been greatly affected.

Over hundreds of years, the technology of the fishing industry has become very sophisticated. During the next decade, the emphasis must be on how to use that technology responsibly to help rebuild and sustain this valuable resource.

Underutilized Species

Newfoundland fish have always been exported to many places around the world, including India, Spain, Japan, Brazil and the West Indies. For centuries the St. John's harbour has bustled with the activity of foreign vessels. The decline of the cod stocks means that new markets must be developed using other, less popular, species. People around the world have different dietary customs

Fish plant at Burin

and preferences. For decades, only foreign trawlers have taken species such as herring and dogfish. These and other kinds of seafood, including lobster, crab, shrimp and turbot, could be the basis of a new Newfoundland fishery.

New markets will have to be found, however, and this means promoting seafood dishes made from a variety of underutilized species ranging from shark and swordfish to shellfish such as periwinkle, sea cucumber and soft-shell clam. Other products, including seaweeds such as kelp, Irish moss and dulse, are already being harvested for an eager market.

Aquaculture

While aquaculture (fish-farming) is an established business worldwide, it is still in an early development stage in Newfoundland. Inshore fisherfolk are being trained to raise cod for cultivation. By far the biggest and most successful aquafarms in the province today are in the commercial mussel industry. Fifty active mussel farms operate on the island, with the biggest ones located in Bay d'Espoir. Salmon, scallops and steelhead trout are being farmed commercially in Notre Dame Bay and Daniel's Harbour. In Wesleyville, experimental stations for marine fin fish are growing rapidly. One station, sponsored by local development associations, is also looking at ways to culture wolf fish and eel pout (a small saltwater fish).

The fishery, as Newfoundlanders and Labradorians have known it, will never be the same. Its very survival will be a challenge, but challenges are nothing new to Newfoundland and Labrador. Already the province is becoming a recognized leader worldwide in marine sciences and in ocean technology that will find applications all over the world.

CHAPTER 8
Enterprise and Initiative

For centuries, the economy of Newfoundland was almost completely dependent on the fisheries. But the province has been blessed with a wealth of other resources — vast forests, rich mineral deposits, offshore oil fields, enormous hydroelectric potential. For some time now, these resources have been playing an ever more important role in the province's economy. In fact, mining surpassed fishing in the dollar value of production some time ago.

The real growth, however, has been in the service industries. Today, over 70 percent of employed people work in service fields such as transportation, finance, trade, health care and tourism.

Transportation and Communication

Powered by paddles and wind, boats and ships of many shapes and sizes were the first forms of transportation around the island. Later on, steam- and diesel-powered vessels plied Newfoundland and Labrador waters. At one time, coastal ships were virtually the only way of getting visitors and supplies to outport communities. While alternative means of transportation exist today, government-subsidized coastal boats still connect many outports.

On land, the forms of transportation vary greatly. For a long time, if someone asked how you were getting from one place to another, you might answer "on shank's mare." That reply simply meant that you were getting there on your own two feet. The first roads on the island were built in 1825, but they were few and far between. By 1963, there were still only 725 kilometres (450 miles) of paved

The business section of St. John's, which remains the commercial heart of the province

73

highway. Today the province has an 8200-kilometre (6000-mile) system of primary and secondary roads, three-quarters of it paved.

The Newfie Bullet

Spurred by the interest in new land for settlement and the search for valuable minerals, construction began on the Newfoundland Railway in 1881. Three years later, the first line was complete from St. John's to Harbour Grace, and in 1898 the first cross-country train left St. John's for Port aux Basques. For almost a hundred years the *Newfie Bullet* (an ironic nickname for a train that was once described as "the slowest crack passenger train in civilization") faithfully wended its way across the island. Its misadventures with snow and winds became legendary, but it played an important role in opening up the interior.

Running a railway over such vast empty stretches was expensive, however. The Newfoundland government took control of the railway in 1923 and ran it until 1949, then passed it over to Canadian National Railways. In 1988, CN pulled up its track and

The Newfie Bullet made its first excursion run from St. John's to Topsail on June 29, 1882.

replaced the Newfie Bullet with a trans-island bus service. The only railway in the province now is the Quebec North Shore and Labrador, which connects the mining area of Labrador with the St. Lawrence port of Sept-Îles.

Air Travel

As North America's closest point to Europe, the province has played a role in the history of air transportation. Just after the First World War, an English newspaper offered a $50 000 prize for the first non-stop flight across the Atlantic. On June 14, 1919, two British officers, Captain John Alcock and Lieutenant Arthur Whitten Brown, took off from Lester's Field in St. John's. They landed in a bog in Clifden, Ireland, 16 hours and 12 minutes later.

Airfields at Gander and Goose Bay were extremely important in ferrying air crews and planes to Europe during the Second World War. Today several airlines fly daily to and from St. John's and other airports in the province. Helicopters also provide emergency service across the province, flying in medical personnel, or evacuating the ill and injured to hospital. Air service is particularly important to the remote communities of Labrador.

A helicopter lands at the Hope Brook Mine campsite.

A Historic Role in Communications

Newfoundland's location also gave it a place in the history of communications. As early as 1851, attempts were made to lay a 2500-kilometre (1600-mile) telegraph cable under the Atlantic Ocean from Europe to Newfoundland. A cable connected in 1858 carried the first transatlantic message, but it failed shortly afterwards. It was successfully reconnected in 1866 at Heart's Content in Trinity Bay. A cable station operated from there until 1965.

In 1901, the Italian inventor Guglielmo Marconi received the first transatlantic wireless message, the letter *S*, at Signal Hill, St. John's. However, the governor, Sir Cavendish Boyle, had been convinced by the transatlantic cable company that the wireless would put them out of business, and so he discouraged Marconi's experiments. Marconi dismantled his invention and left to pursue its development elsewhere.

Farming

Farming in this province has never been easy. Very little of the soil is suitable for agriculture. To make matters worse, the growing season is short and there is less sunshine than many crops need. Still, right from the beginning, settlers made determined efforts to grow things. Traditionally, each family had a kitchen garden supplying vegetables that were stored in underground root cellars.

In spite of the difficulties, commercial farming is on the upswing, with the growth of the industry well above the Canadian average. Prime farm land is being protected by the provincial Department of Agriculture, which also promotes agricultural awareness and provides assistance to farmers through such services as soil testing, crop advice and a regional veterinary service.

Newfoundland is now self-sufficient in milk and egg production. Over the past decade, farms in the fertile Codroy Valley of western Newfoundland have begun to supply vegetables and fruit to supermarkets that once had to depend on mainland and American

Left: Farm in the Codroy Valley, the province's major agricultural area. *Bottom left:* Newfoundland produce on display at the Churchill Square Market in St. John's. *Below:* Sheep farm in western Newfoundland

produce. A wide variety of vegetables such as potatoes, turnips, carrots, beets and broccoli are now locally grown. Recently, sui choy, bok choy and other Chinese vegetables have become popular.

Harvesting wild berries — in particular blueberries, strawberries, partridgeberries and bakeapples — provides extra income for many people. In recent years, careful management of blueberry fields has produced yields of over a million kilograms (2.2 million pounds), much of which is exported. Strawberries are cultivated as well as gathered wild, and the demand for them has encouraged small fruit farmers to expand.

In the mid-1980s, the government tried to develop a cucumber industry using an experimental greenhouse technology. After three years, the project had to be abandoned as impractical.

Right: Loading timber at Goose Bay. Exploitation of Labrador's forest resources remains relatively minor and geared basically to local needs. *Far right:* Corner Brook, Newfoundland's second city, with the pulp and paper mill that is the cornerstone of its economy in the foreground

Forestry

As settlers moved into the interior of the island early in this century, they found an abundance of black spruce and balsam fir, which are ideal for making paper. A new industry was born.

The first paper mill opened in 1909 in Grand Falls and was soon followed by mills in Corner Brook and Stephenville. Today, the Grand Falls, Corner Brook and Stephenville plants account for 75 percent of all revenue generated by the forest sector. When the processing of forest products is included, this sector accounted for almost a quarter of the provincial economy in 1990. Exports of newsprint are shipped throughout North America and even to Asia, Africa and Australia.

Other forest products, such as sawn lumber, particle board and firewood are used locally. Some 2000 licensed sawmills scattered across the province supply up to 50 percent of Newfoundland's lumber needs. Woodworking plants make a variety of products, from doors and cabinets to roof trusses and veneered plywood.

Mining

Mining has long been one of Newfoundland's chief industries. The first copper mine opened in 1867 in Shoal Bay. By the 1920s,

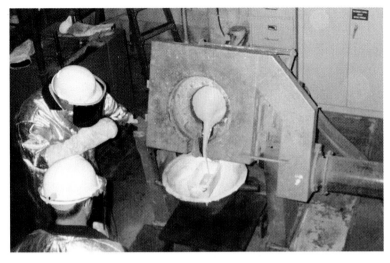

First gold pour at Hope Brook, July 1992

Buchans, near Red Indian Lake, was a thriving mining town with rich deposits of zinc, copper and lead that would secure its future for over 50 years. Bell Island, just a 30-minute ferry ride from St. John's, once contained the largest and richest deposits of iron ore in the world. By 1937, two million tonnes of ore had been mined, but decreasing markets for the type of ore found there forced the closure of the mine in 1966.

The first gold mines in production date back to 1903, but by far the biggest gold deposits were discovered at Hope Brook near Port aux Basques in 1983. The first gold bar was poured there in July 1992. That year, gold production rose to about 120 000 ounces valued at $50 million. This is certainly one of the growth areas in the province and has attracted numerous outsiders seeking their fortune.

The value of mineral production in 1993 reached $707 million. All told, over a dozen minerals are mined, including gypsum, asbestos and limestone. The industry employs about 3000 workers.

Labrador's Mineral Wealth

The formation of the Canadian Shield millions of years ago produced one of nature's happy accidents: an enormous iron ore channel that runs southeastward from Ungava Bay into western Labrador. The Labrador deposit was discovered around 1890, but wasn't developed until the 1950s when the Quebec North Shore and Labrador Railway was built. Between 1975 and 1980, mines at Wabush and Labrador City produced $257 million worth of iron ore. In 1992 the main producer, the Iron Ore Company of Canada, employed 1745 people despite a downturn in mineral prices.

Prospectors continue to look for indicator minerals that might result in diamond mining near Makkovik. Other important Labrador minerals are labradorite, quartz, garnet, agate, chert and marble. Labradorite, a semi-precious stone, is the province's official mineral. It is said that the Native people of Labrador attributed mystical qualities to this beautiful stone because of its captivating play of colours, or *labradorescence*.

Oil Exploration

Oil refineries at Holyrood, Conception Bay and Come By Chance have produced fuel from oil. However, Newfoundland's real potential in oil and gas lies offshore on the Grand Banks. Over the past 25 years, billions of dollars have been spent developing 20 significant oil and gas finds, with 138 wells spudded or drilled. Hibernia, one of Canada's major fields, contains 615 million barrels of oil. It is slated to begin production in 1997 and to yield 12 percent of Canada's light crude oil by the year 2000.

Economic Realities

Newfoundlanders and Labradorians pay the highest taxes in the country, but there is not enough revenue to cover necessary government expenditures. Providing basic services to a small population spread over a large area is difficult and costly. The funding of universities, highways and hospitals is a heavy burden on taxpayers in a province where work is sometimes hard to find. Goods brought from outside the province — as many are — tend to

Oil refinery at Come by Chance. The giant complex went into production in 1973, only to close three years later because of huge operating deficits. It re-opened in 1987. *Inset:* Students launch a rescue tank at the Institute of Marine Dynamics.

be expensive. The recessions of the mid-eighties and early nineties and, especially, the collapse of the fishery have hurt Newfoundland and Labrador and will continue to do so for a while.

Newfoundlanders, however, have some advantages in tough economic times. Seventy percent of them own their own homes, compared to 55 percent of Canadians as a whole. The forests help heat many of these homes, and sea and land still provide sustenance. In many outports a vegetable garden is a common sight. Often home freezers are full of fish, wild game and berries collected during the summer months. As well, the population is more stable than that of many other parts of the country, and people have a wide network of family and community support.

Social Safety Nets
National social programs, such as equalization grants and pensions for seniors, have helped the province overcome the high cost of living in a relatively remote part of the country. Medicare, supported

by federal funding, provides important services, from simple cottage clinics in communities like St. Lawrence to well-equipped hospitals such as the Health Sciences Centre of Memorial University and The Janeway, a hospital for sick children.

With official unemployment traditionally higher than anywhere else in Canada, many Newfoundlanders rely on Canada's Unemployment Insurance program. UIC helps workers who have lost their jobs because of plant or business closures, or because there just is no work. When UIC first came to the province with Confederation, busloads of people came from around the bay to line up at the unemployment office. Working for your stamps, or getting enough work weeks to qualify for UIC benefits, became a way of life for many people. This has been true particularly for workers in the fishery, many of whom are unable to earn enough to support a family during the fishing season. But demand for mineral products and newsprint tends to fluctuate, and periodic plant shutdowns and layoffs in these industries are fairly common.

Government has also established special programs such as DREE (Department of Regional and Economic Expansion) in the 1970s and ACOA (Atlantic Canada Opportunities Agency) to create jobs and provide incentives for young people. Still, there are more Newfoundlanders living in Toronto than in St. John's, and the oil industry drew thousands of Newfoundlanders to Alberta in the 1980s.

On the other hand, new people are coming into the province, some from faraway places such as Bulgaria, Lebanon and Africa, bringing with them fresh ideas and new ways. And the Economic Recovery Commission, set up in 1991, has launched local industry and consumer initiatives to promote the province. Developing pride and a positive outlook is a step in the right direction.

Into the Future

If the old saying, "Necessity is the mother of invention," holds true, Newfoundland and Labrador will have a great future. St. John's is now a leader in marine research. As a division of the National Research Council (NRC), the Institute of Marine Dynamics has developed expertise in cold ocean and marine ice research. Its facilities, including a ship simulator, are also used to train naval officers in vessel manoeuvring. Many of the complex instruments are designed and made at the Institute.

Over 700 Newfoundland companies are now manufacturing non-resource based products ranging from fabricated metal products to satellite communications equipment. In recent years, they have supplied many goods and services to Canada's Department of National Defence, such as army boots, environmental and engineering consulting services, and the refitting of naval vessels. There is growing interest in manufacturing aerospace equipment, and there has been some remarkable success in the production of computer software and in medical care innovations. What's next to invent or manufacture will be limited only by future demand.

Environmental Challenges

With change, especially in technology and industry, has come a growing awareness of its impact on the environment. Government, public interest groups and individuals are seeking to take better care of the earth. The biggest challenge is to reduce the effects of mistakes already made and to avoid new mistakes in the future.

The development of the oil industry poses a constant threat of oil spills that are damaging to seabirds and ocean life. To prepare for such disasters, oil companies have an environmental agreement to clean up any spills and cover the costs of replacing bird habitats. Logging has also affected wildlife, and there are several endangered species in the province. The population of the Newfoundland marten, an indigenous small animal, has fallen to about 300. The piping plover, a robin-sized shorebird, now has its own Recovery Team working to prevent its extinction.

An essential step in protecting the environment is to change the way resources are used. Forest management, for example, is now a major issue not just for concerned individuals, but for the industry itself. Old practices have contributed to erosion, and pesticides used to protect the commercial value of the forest may have long-term health risks. There is a constant danger from forest fires and, in some areas, from over-cutting for fuel. To help combat this problem, reforestation programs have been developed in such places as Salmonier Line, where a million trees are planted annually.

Local Action on the Environment

People in Newfoundland and Labrador, like everyone else, have a garbage problem. Even the best efforts to get people to reduce, reuse, recycle and compost solid waste leave a lot to be disposed of some other way. Landfill — creating huge heaps of garbage and covering them over with soil — is not really practical in much of the province because the soil is so shallow. Incineration has been used, but the technology is dated and air emissions are of great concern. The Atlantic Coast Action Plan (ACAP) has made the improvement of incinerator plants one of its main objectives.

In 1992, an American company proposed bringing in 3500 tonnes of garbage a day from New York to be burned in a new incinerator in Long Harbour, Placentia Bay. The incinerator, which would also generate electricity, would be the largest in North America. Although it would be a boost to Long Harbour's economy, there have been public protests about the plan. Environmental groups believe incineration creates air and water pollution and may attract rodents and plant life not normally found here. SNAGG (Say No To American Garbage Group) is a public action group that has called for a careful look at the long-term implications of the project.

Other groups have been formed to help clean up our waters and preserve fish stocks. FLOW (Friends and Lobbyists of the Waterford River) and the Quidi Vidi Rennies River Development Foundation have launched an extensive public awareness campaign to improve the condition of the waterways. The dumping of toxic chemicals and raw sewage into the water system that flows directly into the ocean is a major problem. The Newfoundland and Labrador Environment Network keeps the public informed through a newsletter and workshops. The Salmon Council of Newfoundland and the Protected Areas Association are just two of the other citizen groups working to protect the environment for future generations.

Local companies are recognizing the value of the province's resources and the importance of environmentally friendly products. Some are establishing recycling businesses for plastic, paper, glass and aluminum. There is much still to do, however, if we are to reduce the amount of waste we create. This definitely will be everyone's challenge into the next century.

Left: "Electro-fishing" on a tributary of the Waterford River. Electro-fishing is a method of monitoring the fish population of a stream. *Right:* Tree nursery

CHAPTER 9

Culture and Recreation

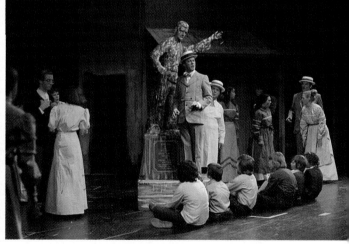

The people of Newfoundland and Labrador know how to kick up their heels and have a good time or spontaneously tell a yarn than can leave you in stitches. A love for their own culture has inspired a strong storytelling and songwriting tradition. Language is a significant part of that culture. Numerous speech patterns and accents truly set Newfoundland and Labrador apart from other Canadian provinces. Hundreds of dialects, especially in the outports, are as rich as any poem and as lyrical as any song.

Music and Storytelling

Telling stories and putting them to music are important ways in which Newfoundanders stay in touch with their heritage and pass it on from one generation to another. There is a strong legacy of Irish, Scottish and English traditions here that have influenced many festive events. One of the most colourful is mummering. A Christmastime activity, mummering traditionally involved people disguising themselves in costumes and performing a play, parading through the streets or going from house to house singing and dancing. While mummering is not as common as it once was (it was actually banned in the nineteenth century), the house visiting is still popular in several outports. As well, modern theatre groups are reviving the Mummer's Play tradition.

Clockwise from top left: **The St. John's Regatta; folksinger Ron Hynes, whose popular recordings include the 1993 CD** *Cryer's Paradise;* **the St. John's Arts and Culture Centre's production of** *The Music Man,* **with Gordon Pinsent; sculpture entitled** *Natural Gas* **by Inuit artist Gilbert Hay. Hay's works, which often explore the effects of mainstream Canadian society on Inuit culture, are found in many public, corporate and private collections.**

Over the years, there have been many great storytellers and songwriters. In the 1930s, Johnny Burke was dubbed "the bard of Prescott Street." He stood on corners singing his songs and selling sheets of his music. Today, Ron Hynes is well known for singing original compositions such as his international hit "Sonny's Dream."

Interest is growing in traditional forms of music, from the fiddling and accordion playing of old-timers like Emile Benoit and Rufus Guinchard to the playing of spoons and the mandolin. Many Newfoundlanders are enthusiastically taking private lessons from fiddlers and other traditional musicians, and Memorial University's credit courses in traditional music are growing in popularity.

In popular music, The Ravens' song "Young Blood" was a big hit in the 1960s. One of the earliest traditional/rock groups, The Wonderful Grand Band, had a record-breaking television audience for their show, *The Root Seller*. It was here that well-known guitarist Sandy Morris and other musicians, such as Noel Dinn, helped re-establish traditional music as the foundation of present-day trends.

Part of the mummering tradition involves guessing who the disguised visitors are. If the hosts succeed, the mummers must remove their masks.

The 1990s saw The Thomas Trio and the Red Albino rise to popularity, and the traditional/modern group Figgy Duff has released several successful CDs and videos. Other popular musicians are Anita Best and Pamela Morgan, whose CD *The Colour of Amber* won first prize at the 1993 East Coast Music Awards.

Folk Festivals

Each summer there are as many as 25 folk festivals held across the province, often sponsored by local service clubs or town councils. Among these are the Carbonear Folk Festival, the Ferryland Folk Festival and the Folk Arts Festival in St. John's, all celebrating traditional and modern music. These events often include a display of local crafts, and sometimes feature a *jiggs dinner,* a *Newfie scoff* of boiled vegetables, salt beef and figgy pudding. The success of these festivals has meant that performers can spend several weeks in the summer travelling from one community to another.

Far left: **Legendary fiddler Emile Benoit in an August 1991 performance.**
Left: **The Thomas Trio and the Red Albino, one of the most popular rock bands of the early nineties.**

Right: St. John's Day celebrations in the capital. *Far right:* Newfoundland's francophones celebrate their roots at Une Longue Veillée, a summer festival of music, dance, story telling and crafts.

The annual Kiwanis Music Festival celebrates the talents of young musicians and vocalists. One of the best-known choirs is the Holy Heart of Mary Choir. Its unique harmony and presentation have led to a number of invitations, including one from Carnegie Hall in New York.

Dance and Theatre

Square dancing is popular in Newfoundland and Labrador, particularly at a *time*, a large community party. An accordion player and a fiddler usually provide the musical accompaniment as people shout and stamp their feet through the complicated patterns of the dance. Step dancing is another well-loved and traditional type of dancing, often performed alone or holding hands with another dancer. It is very fast and often done in double time. These dances have always been popular here and continue to attract the interest of young people.

Classical ballet and modern dance are relatively new to Newfoundland culture, but there are several dance schools, as well as professional companies such as Neighbourhood Dance Works.

Left: The Nicole Nogaret Classical Dance School. *Bottom left:* Mr. Masterminder, alias Beni Malone, Newfoundland's only professional clown. Beni has entertained thousands of children, often travelling by boat to the remote corners of the province. *Below:* CODCO

Newfoundlanders have a great sense of humour and love to laugh. Each year Rising Tide Theatre's Review Show takes a satirical look at political and public events of the past year. The nationally famous CODCO troupe has spent the last 20 years performing plays and skits that poke fun at everything and everyone. The CODCO members write all their own material, and while they are often hilarious, they also raise serious questions about issues important to Newfoundlanders.

The Resource Centre for the Arts in St. John's is an artist-run theatre and art gallery. Located in the historic Long Shoreman's Protection Union Hall, the Centre has been producing original theatre featuring local performers and directors such as Janis Spence, Greg Thomey and Lois Brown with much success. Troupes like Sheilagh's Brush have performed here, as have individual performers such as Rick Mercer and Andrew Younghusband.

The Provincial Drama Festival offers young artists the opportunity to test their skills and have them judged by professionals. The Newfoundland and Labrador Arts Council assists artists financially, and in 1992 the Federal-Provincial Cooperation Agreement was established to develop and promote the work of artists.

Film and Television

Actor Gordon Pinsent, among others, has helped bring Newfoundland to the attention of the rest of Canada with such productions as *The Rowdyman* and *John and the Missus.* Local film and video productions are rapidly taking centre stage. NIFCO, Newfoundland Independent Filmmakers Co-op, has backed several works, including *Secret Nation*, a fictitious account of events leading up to Confederation with Canada. *The Boys of St. Vincent*, a film based on the tragic abuse of young boys at a Newfoundland orphanage, won an award at the Cannes Film Festival in France in 1992.

Visual Art and Crafts

Challenged by the dramatic and rugged nature of the province, many artists strive to capture the landscape and the people who live here. Mary Pratt, Christopher Pratt, David Blackwood, Rae Perlin, Gerald Squires and Lise Sorensen are just a few of the artists who find inspiration in this place. Their works vary widely. For instance, Gerald Squires paints detailed landscapes, while Mary Pratt transforms everyday household objects into vibrant works of art. The Memorial University Art Gallery has an important permanent collection of local artists' works.

Isolated by the North Atlantic, settlers and colonists had to master the skills necessary for survival and comfort. Their success is still evident today, even though people no longer depend on handmade goods for their basic needs. Crafts by Newfoundland weavers, knitters, quilters, carvers, woodworkers, metalworkers and tanners are famous for their practicality and unique designs.

Old techniques, such as thrummed knitting, brought by early English settlers, are enjoying a revival. Tufts of wool are knit into hats, mitts and socks to create a warm lining. Metalsmiths once forged vital pieces of equipment, and they still do; but today they also make lovely jewellery, sometimes set with rare labradorite gemstone. Tea-dolls of Labrador have a delightful origin. When Innu bands travelled on the land, it was customary for everyone to help out. Small children carried traditionally dressed dolls — stuffed with tea leaves. After the tea was used up, the dolls were re-stuffed with grass or straw.

The Craft Development Association hosts three displays each year of local craftspeople's work, including pottery, which is a relatively new craft in the province. In 1993, an abandoned Salvation Army church in Carbonear was converted into a studio where potters mould island clay into vases, pots and dishware.

Above: Uncle Cluny's Kite over Wesleyville, etching by David Blackwood. *Left:* Hooked mat by Lois Saunders. Once valued only as something to wipe your feet on, handmade hooked mats now adorn the walls of many art collectors.

Creative Writing

There have always been great writers in this province, such as the poet E.J. Pratt, who won three Governor General's awards. His *Newfoundland Verse* is a haunting yet fiercely realistic evocation of Newfoundland life. But many writers were not recognized nationally for a long time. One of the province's first successful novelists, Margaret Duley, was read in the United States and Britain long before she was acknowledged at home. However, things have changed, and the works of local authors now share shelf space with those of other renowned Canadian writers. Helen Fogwill Porter has won awards for her young adult novel, *January, February, June or July*. Kevin Major's book *Hold Fast* is on the curriculum in schools in other provinces (although not in his own). Novels by Wayne Johnson, Harold Horwood, Joan Clark, Percy Janes, and poetry by John Steffler have been praised by critics, and the witty comments of satirist Ray Guy reach a large, appreciative audience.

Several writers' groups have emerged over the last decade. The Writers' Alliance of Newfoundland and Labrador is broad-based, representing both established and new writers, while the small East Coast Women and Words works to assist feminist writers.

Recreation and Sport

The annual St. John's Regatta is the oldest sporting event in North America. The first rowing teams competed on a 2.6-kilometre (1.6-mile) course on Quidi Vidi Lake from as early as 1826. Held the first Wednesday of August (or the next fine day), this event draws thousands of people each year.

Hockey, curling and skiing are popular winter sports, and recreational sailing and rowing have always been enjoyed in summer. Baseball and soccer teams play throughout the province.

Provincial athletes have participated successfully in many national and international competitions. Joy Burt, who has been called the strongest woman in the world in her weight class, won the world power-lifting championship in 1992. Paul Merlo and Pam Ennis are diving stars, while swimmers Blair Tucker and Ian Tennant and wrestler Chris Valers have won gold at the Canada Games. In 1993, Travis King became the first Newfoundlander to win a silver medal for high-bar gymnastics at the national championship meet. Mel FitzGerald and JoAnn McDonald are world-champion wheelchair athletes. At the Special Olympics in Austria in March 1993, Wayne Maloney won gold and Leslie Ann Durdle won silver in cross-country skiing. One unusual Newfoundland champion is Carolyn Hayward of St. John's, who was an internationally renowned bullfighter in the 1960s.

Much to the delight of hockey fans, the St. John's Maple Leafs brought professional sports to the province. Several broadcasters have received national acclaim. Bob Cole, a Hockey Night in Canada play-by-play broadcaster, is a household name during hockey season, and Suzanne Blake is the first woman sports broadcaster for CBC national radio.

Left: Yacht race off Bell Island. *Above:* Wayne Maloney and Leslie Ann Durdle training for the 1993 Special Olympics

CHAPTER 10

Around the Province

Opposite page – top: Skiers at Marble Mountain. *Centre:* Solitary camper enjoying the magnificent scenery of the island's west coast. *Bottom left:* A trio of young Newfoundlanders in St. John's. *Bottom right:* A new and charming role for a barking kettle, traditionally used for preserving fishnets by boiling them with tree bark. *Above, clockwise from top right:* Several species of whales visit Newfoundland's coastal waters; iceberg inTrinity Bay; North-West River, Labrador; the south coast outport of François

Newfoundland and Labrador attracts increasing numbers of visitors each year. They come to enjoy the rugged scenery and warm hospitality, the clean water and air, the relaxed pace and the rich cultural heritage of the people.

All too often, however, visitors "from away" see little more than St. John's and the Avalon Peninsula.This is a shame since the province's potential is barely tapped. Still, the Avalon area is a good place from which to start a tour of the province.

The Avalon Area

In St. John's, visitors can enjoy scenic trails along Rennie's River and look out across the Atlantic from Signal Hill. A walk along the Hill, or through the old part of the city, provides glimpses of Newfoundland's past. Harbour tours offer a dramatically different view of the city, and boat tours can take the more adventurous whale watching, kayaking and sailing.

Downtown St. John's is dotted with colourful wooden houses painted in individual styles. As one might expect, there are many interesting historic buildings, including the white limestone Colonial Building, now home to the Provincial Archives; the Roman Catholic Basilica of St. John the Baptist with its 42-metre (138-feet) high twin spires; and the Anglican Cathedral of St. John the Baptist, which experts say is the best example of Gothic church architecture in North America.

Water Street, the commercial hub of the city for more than 400 years, bustles with shops, pubs, restaurants, boutiques, art galleries and museums. The Newfoundland Museum features artifacts from

Clockwise from top left: The brightly painted wooden houses of old St. John's; the St. John's War Memorial; hot dog stand in downtown St. John's; the Memorial University Botanical Garden, which features a unique blend of cultivated flower gardens and a variety of natural habitats

Native peoples as well as collections from the island's long history. The Arts and Culture Centre, built in 1967 as a Canadian centennial project, houses the Memorial University of Newfoundland Art Gallery, a large auditorium and several small theatre spaces.

Out Around the Bay

A trip "out around the bay," leads to the question, "Which bay?" Should it be Conception Bay, Trinity Bay, St. Mary's Bay or Placentia Bay? Preferably all of them, because each one has its own charm and its own sights to be seen, from the gravestone of Sheila Na Geira at Carbonear, the ruins of French fortifications at Placentia and the old Cable Station at Heart's Content to cliffs alive with seabirds at Cape St. Mary's and fossils of sea creatures that lived over 600 000 years ago at Mistaken Point.

One community slightly off the beaten track is Brigus on Conception Bay. It was here that Rockwell Kent, the famous American artist, established a summer home and studio. It is also the birthplace of Captain Bob Bartlett, one of the outstanding pioneers of navigation in the Arctic. His former home, Hawthorne Cottage, has been declared a historic site. Among other special features of Brigus are stone buildings, rock walls that serve as fences and a stunning view from its sheltered bay.

Bay de Verde, a fishing community near the tip of the peninsula that separates Trinity Bay and Conception Bay, was originally settled in the 1600s. *Inset:* **Winter in Brigus South**

The old lighthouse at Cape Spear. Built in 1835 on the most easterly point of land in North America, this is the island's oldest surviving lighthouse — but it almost wasn't. Slated for demolition when a new one was built, it was saved at the last minute by public protest. *Inset:* The ruggedness of the island's coastline means that really good, accessible beaches — like this one on Conception Bay — are rather few and far between.

Eastern Region

West across Trinity Bay from the Avalon Peninsula, lies the Bonavista Peninsula. About three-quarters of the way along its east coast is Trinity, a national heritage community steeped in Newfoundland history. Legend credits Portuguese explorer Gaspar Corte-Real with naming the site in honour of Trinity Sunday, the day he arrived. Once an important fishing and mercantile community, the old town has many impressive nineteenth-century homes, testament to its former prosperity. In St. Paul's Anglican Church, it also has what many consider the loveliest small church on the island.

At the tip of the peninsula is windswept Cape Bonavista with its historic lighthouse and its monument to John Cabot. About a third of the way around Bonavista Bay, Terra Nova National Park beckons local and visiting nature lovers. It is an area of sheltered bays, dense forests, wildflower-strewn bogs and varied wildlife, including arctic tern, osprey, eagles, lynx, black bear and moose.

At this point, travellers might want to head southwest to visit old fishing centres such as Frenchman's Cove, English Harbour East and Spanish Room on the Burin Peninsula. At Fortune, a ferry makes regular crossings to the islands of St. Pierre and Miquelon, France's last North American territories. From Terrenceville, at the head of Fortune Bay, the adventurous can take the ferry that services isolated south coast communities such as English Harbour West, Harbour Breton, Ramea and Burgeo.

Clockwise from top left: **Dory races at Garden Cove on the Burin Peninsula; St. Paul's Anglican Church, Trinity — some of the headstones in the graveyard date back 250 years; the pretty community of Charlottetown, once a lumbering centre for Bonavista Bay, now primarily a vacation centre; the Southern Newfoundland Seamen's Museum at Grand Bank**

Central Newfoundland

The heart of central Newfoundland contains vast stands of spruce, birch and pine. Here the Beothuk first lived; later the burgeoning lumber and paper industries drew settlers. The banks of Newfoundland's longest river, the Exploits, lead upriver past the towns of Lewisporte, Bishop's Falls and Grand Falls-Windsor. Small, clapboard houses hug the rocks, bays and inlets along the Atlantic coast, Hamilton Sound and Notre Dame Bay. Life here is close to the earth, the pace is slower and the people always seem to have time for a chat.

The Mary March Museum in Grand Falls documents Native history, European exploration and the natural history of the area. In Notre Dame Bay, a short ferry ride from Farewell, lie the Change Islands, a place where, ironically, little has changed since the last century. The first car arrived here in 1965! The larger island of Fogo has been designated as one of the four corners of the world by the

Left: **Fogo Island in Notre Dame Bay was first settled in the 1680s.** *Below:* **Reconstruction of a** *mamateek* **at the Beothuk Village in Grand Falls – Windsor**

Right: Canadian Coast Guard cutter in the harbour at Twillingate. *Far Right:* The west coast of Bonavista Bay is famous for its seafarers. One of them, Captain Benjamin Barbour, built this handsome 32-room house at Newtown over 100 years ago.

Flat Earth Society. Many old folk customs from England survive here. Much of the folklore of Newfoundland began in this part of the island and inspired traditional songs like "Ise the Bye" ("I'm the boy....").

The coastal community of Twillingate, on New World Island, was once the centre of the fishing industry in the area. It is also the home of the famous opera singer Georgina Stirling, known professionally as Marie Toulinguet. The town maintains its history in the beautifully preserved Twillingate Museum, formerly the Anglican Rectory. Here are historic photographs, tools, artifacts of the Maritime Archaic Indians and rooms that show what a turn-of-the-century house of means looked like.

The West Coast

Western Newfoundland has some of the most spectacular scenery in the province. Visitors arriving by ferry at Channel–Port aux Basques are at the site of what was once an important fishing town for French, Portuguese and Basques. The road northward passes through fertile valleys with the Long Range Mountains on one side and the Gulf of St. Lawrence on the other. An awesome beauty mixes with the eerie atmosphere of Table Mountain, where gale force winds have been known to quite literally take one's breath away. On St. George's Bay is Stephenville, the site of the American

Top: A riot of wildflowers and breathtaking views are just two of the many delights Gros Morne National Park offers summer visitors. *Left:* Lark Harbour, at the southern entrance to the Bay of Islands. *Above:* The Arches, one of many unusual rock formations the sea has created along the coast of the Great Northern Peninsula

Harmon Air Force Base, built during the Second World War. Today Stephenville has its own airport and supports much small industry. Each summer the Stephenville Festival presents a slate of plays ranging from works by local playwrights to Broadway hits. A side trip along the Port au Port Peninsula provides an introduction to the province's French heritage.

Corner Brook, nestled between the Long Range Mountains and the Humber River, is the province's west coast city. In winter, the place bustles with a carnival centred on Marble Mountain, which offers some of the best skiing in Atlantic Canada. At any time of the year, horseback riding and hiking take the curious through the unforgettable scenery of the Bay of Islands and the Humber River. At Curling, a monument displays copies of the maps Captain James Cook made of the coast of Newfoundland between 1763 and 1767.

A trip from Deer Lake to the tip of the Great Northern Peninsula is a journey into the province's ancient past. Gros Morne National

Park has been named a UNESCO World Heritage Site because of its unique natural beauty and its ancient geological landscape. Farther north along the peninsula is Port au Choix, the site of burial grounds of the Maritime Archaic Indians. Nearby are excavations from an early Dorset community. At the very tip of the Peninsula is the only known site of Norse settlement in North America — L'Anse aux Meadows — where Vikings briefly lived a thousand years ago.

Labrador

There are two ways to visit Labrador by automobile. From St. Barbe on the Great Northern Peninsula, a summer and fall ferry crosses the Strait of Belle Isle to Blanc Sablon, Quebec. An 80-kilometre (50-mile) paved road then leads to Red Bay, where the Basques operated their whaling station in the sixteenth century. Along the way, a must-see is L'Anse-Amour where archaeologists have found evidence of the Maritime Archaic Indians. A series of small campsites and burial grounds are reminders that humans inhabited this area 9000 years ago. Sport fishing is now a major attraction of this area.

Only recently has it been possible to visit western and central Labrador by motor vehicle. A road now connects Baie Comeau on the north shore of the St. Lawrence River to Labrador City and Wabush, where the largest open-pit iron mine in the world operates. Recreational winter sports include excellent downhill and cross-

Winter is, of course, Labrador's most characteristic season, but Labradorians know how to enjoy as well as survive it.

country skiing, as well as dog sledding and snowshoeing. Two World Cup events have been hosted at the Menihek Nordic Ski Club. Eastward along a gravel road is Churchill Falls, where a huge underground generating station pumps over 5000 megawatts of power. The road ends at Happy Valley-Goose Bay, communities that have depended heavily on their role as a military air base. Here, too, recreation has a growing importance. Downhill and cross-country skiing and ice fishing dominate in the winter, while the nearby lakes offer fishing, canoeing and boating in the summer.

Much of Labrador can only be visited by ship. Summer and fall, a coastal boat travels for two weeks from Lewisport to Nain in the Far North and back again, loading and unloading freight in small communities along the way. Limited passenger service is available on the boat. Icebergs are a common sight on this trip. The land and communities visited offer great contrasts — the old fishing community of Battle Harbour, the heavily wooded and relatively new logging community of Port Hope Simpson and Nain, now the most northerly community on the Labrador coast, with its bare rock and barren tundra. At the Nain Museum, visitors can see Inuit artifacts and collections from the Moravian Mission.

"Flightseeing" is another way of seeing Labrador — and, in fact, through much of this part of the province, there is no other means of travel. Hunting, sport fishing and photography are among the reasons for the growing popularity of this form of tourism.

Buttercups and fish shack at L'Anse au Loup in southeastern Labrador

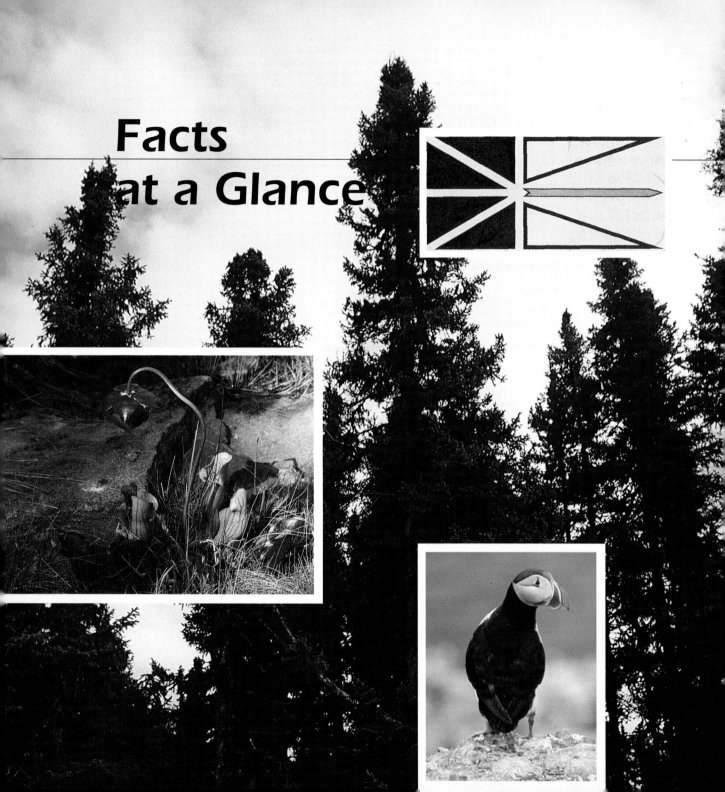

Facts
at a Glance

General Information

Entered Confederation: March 31, 1949

Origin of Name: "New found land" was the name given to the island by early explorers. Labrador may come from the Portuguese "Terra del Lavrador"; *lavrador* means landowner.

Provincial Capital: St. John's

Provincial Nickname: The Rock

Provincial Motto: *Quaerite prime regnum Dei* (Latin for "Seek ye first the Kingdom of God")

Provincial Flower: Pitcher plant

Provincial Tree: Black spruce

Provincial Bird: Puffin

Provincial Tartan: Newfoundland's tartan is green, gold, white, brown and red: green for pine-clad hills, gold for sunlight, white for the snow of winter, brown for iron ore and red for the royal standard of its ancestors.

Provincial Flag: The flag is a red, gold and blue design placed against a background of white. White represents snow and ice, blue represents the sea, red and gold represent confidence in the future.

As well, Labrador has its own white, blue and green flag and a French Newfoundland flag was adopted in 1986.

Population

(1991 census)

Population: 568 475, ninth among Canadian provinces

Population Density: 1.4 persons per km² (3.6 per sq. mi.)

Population Distribution: 58.9% urban and 41.1% rural

Cities and Towns

St. John's	96 200
Corner Brook	22 700
Mount Pearl	20 200
Conception Bay South	15 500
Gander	10 300
Grand Falls	9 100
Labrador City	8 665
Happy Valley-Goose Bay	7 250

Population Growth

1951	361 416
1961	457 853
1971	552 105
1981	567 680
1991	568 475

Ethnic Origin

British	442 805
French	9 700
Inuit	2 670
First Nations	2 350
Chinese	740
Métis	320

Mother Tongue: In the 1991 census, an overwhelming 559 620 or 98.4% of Newfoundlanders and Labradorians claimed English as their mother tongue. Most prominent among other languages mentioned were French (2400), Montagnais-Naskapi (1110), Chinese (735) and Inuktitut (485).

Geography

Borders: The province lies between the 46th and 61st parallels with the bulk of the island below the 50th parallel. The island is located in the Gulf of St. Lawrence, separated from Labrador by the Strait of Belle Isle and from Nova Scotia by the Cabot Strait. Labrador is bordered by Quebec on the west and south.

Overall Area: 404 519 km² (156 185 sq. mi.)

Area of Island: 112 300 km² (43 359 sq. mi.)

Area of Labrador: 292 219 km² (112 826 sq. mi.)

Highest Point: Mount Caubvick, Torngat Mountains, 1652 m (5321 ft.)

Rank in Area Among Provinces: seventh

Rivers and Lakes: Major rivers include Exploits, Gander, Humber and Terra Nova on the island and the Churchill and Naskaupi in Labrador. The Smallwood Reservoir is the largest lake in Labrador, followed by Lake Melville. Grand Lake, Red Indian Lake, Gander Lake and Deer Lake are the largest on the island.

Topography: Labrador is part of the Canadian Shield. The coastal terrain is rocky and barren. The interior is a large plateau drained by many rivers. The jagged Torngat Mountains have been eroded over time by rivers and glaciers. The island, formed from continental drift (North America colliding with Africa) eons ago, has many low-lying valleys as well as mountainous regions. The coastlines of the mainland and the island are ragged with bays and coves.

There are three distinct natural regions. Northern Labrador is tundra with only mosses and stunted shrubs. Southern Labrador is taiga Shield, covered by bogs and barrens. Lichen forests with black spruce are found in better-drained areas. The island is rugged but heavily forested in the valleys and lowlands. Mountainous regions on the west coast have sparser vegetation.

Climate: In northern Labrador, winters are long and bitterly cold. The lowest recorded January temperature is -48°C (-54°F) at Sangirt Lake in 1946, but temperatures in the mountains can be even lower. In the south, along the coast and on the island, the temperatures are somewhat warmer in winter, moderated by the ocean's influence. The average low in January is -7°C (19°F). However, breezes off the cold Labrador Sea also moderate summer temperatures, which average between 10° and 15°C (50° and 59°F). Coastal regions experience a great deal of rainfall and fog. St. John's has an average 1513 mm (60 in.) of precipitation a year.

Nature

Trees: Spruce and balsam fir predominate. Other varieties include white birch, pine, aspen and alder.

Wild Plants and Berries: Bunchberry, corn lily, creeping snowberry, Indian pipe, northeastern rose, bog rosemary, Labrador tea, pitcher plant, blueberry, partridgeberry, bakeapple.

Animals: Mammals include caribou, moose, black bear, lynx, red fox, muskrat, beaver, marten, and several kinds of seals.

Birds: Among the many species of seabirds are gull, gannet, murre, puffin, razor-billed auk and duck. Inland birds include northern flicker, black-capped chickadee, black crow, blue jay, evening grosbeak, woodpecker, hawk and owl.

Fish and shellfish: Saltwater species include cod, turbot, plaice, lobster, herring, mackerel, squid, eel, scallops, shrimp and crab. Freshwater species include brook trout, rainbow trout, brown trout and American eel. Atlantic salmon live most of their life in the sea but spawn in fresh water.

Government

Federal: The province is represented by seven members in the House of Commons and six in the Senate.

Provincial: There are 52 elected members in the House of Assembly. The leader of the political party with the most elected members becomes premier. The premier appoints a cabinet from members of his party, who then head government departments. The premier and the cabinet are called the Executive Council. Voters must be Canadian citizens, 18 years of age and residents of the province for six months.

Local: There are three cities, 170 towns, 140 communities and 110 local service districts. Town and community councils have elected officials with limited powers, while city councils have full authority over local services.

Education

The provincial government funds some 600 schools with a current enrolment of about 140 000 students from kindergarten to grade 12.

A salmon leaps Big Falls, in Squires Memorial Park, on its way to its spawning waters farther up the Humber River.

The province has one university, Memorial University of Newfoundland, with two campuses. The main campus is in St. John's, and the other, Sir Wilfred Grenfell College, is in Corner Brook. About 9800 full-time and 4000 part-time students attend the university. There are also three provincial institutes: Cabot Institute of Applied Arts and Technology and the Institute of Fisheries and Marine Technology in St. John's, and the Fisher Institute of Applied Arts and Technology in Corner Brook. As well, there are five community colleges, each with several regional campuses.

Economy

The fishery was the mainstay of Newfoundland and Labrador's economy for centuries, followed by mining and forestry. Much of the province's industry is still related to processing natural resources. Of those employed, 8 percent work in the primary industries, about 17 percent in secondary or manufacturing industries, and 73 percent in the service sector. The level of unemployment is high.

Principal Products

Fishery: Atlantic salmon, flounder, turbot, halibut, crab, lobster, shrimp, herring. Cod has always been the most important catch, but in 1992 a ban on cod fishing was declared because of depleted stocks.

Forestry: Pulp and paper (newsprint), lumber

Mining and Energy: Iron ore, copper, gold, gypsum, limestone and hydroelectrical power

Agriculture: Root vegetables, blueberries, pigs, dairy cows, sheep, poultry, milk and eggs

Manufacturing: Fish processing, pulp and paper, wood products, marine equipment, medical devices, boatbuilding

Transportation

Ferries run year-round between Channel-Port aux Basques and North Sydney, Nova Scotia, and in summer from Argentia to North Sydney. Ferries also link the island with Labrador and several smaller islands.

The Trans-Canada Highway crosses Newfoundland from Channel-Port aux Basques to St. John's, and there are almost 6000 km (3728 mi.) of paved side roads. Labrador City and Red Bay have Labrador's only direct road links wiht the exterior.

The Stephenville, Gander International and St. John's airports connect the province with major North American and European destinations. Regional airlines use the airports in Happy Valley-Goose Bay, Churchill Falls, Labrador City and Wabush. There are also 27 airstrips and seven heliports.

Communications

There are two dailies, *The Evening Telegram* in St. John's and the *Western Star* in Corner Brook. Community

Life in a 1910 merchant's household is recreated at the restored Hiscock House in Trinity.

newspapers include *The Southern Gazette*, *The Packet*, *The Beacon*, *The Humber Log*, *The Nor-Wester*, *The Gulf News*, *The Northern Pen*. In Labrador, *The Labradorian*, *The Aurora* and *The Northern Reporter* are published weekly. There is one French newspaper on the island, *Le Gaboteur*, published in Stephenville.

The province is served by the national television network of the CBC, private broadcasting, cable television and a satellite service called the Atlantic Satellite Network. The province has CBC radio and several private radio stations.

Social and Cultural Life

Museums: The Newfoundland Museum in St. John's focuses on the history and traditions of the Native peoples and the varied living styles of later settlers. There are many local museums such as the Conception Bay Museum in Harbour Grace, the Southern Newfoundland Seaman's Museum in Grand Bank, the Humber Valley Heritage Museum in Deer Lake and the Labrador Straits Museum in L'Anse au Loup.

Historic Sites and Landmarks

Cape Spear National Historic Park, south of St. John's, is the closest place in North America to Europe. Its lighthouse, built in 1836, is the oldest in Newfoundland and one of the oldest in Canada. It has been restored with turn-of-the-century furnishings.

Captain James Cook Monument offers an impressive view of Corner Brook and the Bay of Islands. Copies are displayed here of original charts made by Captain Cook in 1764.

Castle Hill National Historic Park at Placentia commemorates a site that provided good anchorage and fresh water to early Basque and French fisherfolk. The area was occupied by the French until 1713 and many French fortifications remain.

Gros Morne National Park, 1942 km² (750 sq. mi.) on the western seacoast has been designated a UNESCO World Heritage Site. Its geological wonders include billion-year-old cliffs and deep fjords.

Heart's Content Cable Station on Trinity Bay is a provincial historic site commemorating the place where the first successful transatlantic cable was brought ashore in the 1860s.

L'Anse aux Meadows National Historic Site, a UNESCO World Heritage Site, is on the northern tip of the Great

Northern Peninsula. Here, in the 1960s and 1970s, archaeological excavations uncovered the remains of a Norse settlement dating from about A.D. 1000. Sod houses have been recreated and artifacts are on display.

Port au Choix National Historic Site, on the Great Northern Peninsula, is the site of a burial ground of the Maritime Archaic Indians. Artifacts and the remains of nearly 100 individuals found here have been carbon-dated to between 3200 and 4300 years ago.

Red Bay, on the southern coast of Labrador, is the sixteenth-century site of a Basque whaling station. Archaeologists have found relics of buildings and a cemetery containing the remains of 140 workers and the wreck of a whaling ship, *San Juan.*

Cabot Tower on Signal Hill is one of Canada's best-known landmarks.

Signal Hill National Historic Site and *Cabot Tower* are perched atop a rocky outlook near the mouth of St. John's Harbour. The tower, built in 1897, commemorates John Cabot's arrival in 1497. Guglielmo Marconi received the first transatlantic radio transmission at this site in 1901. Signal Hill was once an important look-out point. Each summer, significant battles are re-enacted here.

Terra Nova National Park, 400 km^2 (154 sq. mi.) of protected area on the southwest side of Bonavista Bay offers hiking and nature trails as well as interpretive exhibits that explain the park's plants and wildlife.

Trinity is a national heritage community with several sites and homes restored and furnished to their original period. Walking trails lead to wildflower meadows and breathtaking views of the land and sea.

Other Interesting Places to Visit

Bell Island, in Conception Bay, is a short ferry ride from St. John's. Murals painted on the exterior walls of several buildings depict life on the island earlier this century.

Cape St. Mary's, in the southeastern part of Newfoundland, is an important ecological reserve. It is the second largest nesting site for gannets in North America and a nursery for thousands of murres and kittiwakes.

Freshwater Resource Centre in St. John's houses the only public fluvarium in North America. Through nine windows, visitors can observe trout and arctic char in their natural environment. The centre also contains exhibits, aquariums and displays of freshwater ecology.

Grenfell House in St. Anthony was the home of medical missionary Sir Wilfred Grenfell. Built in the early 1900s, the house features an exhibit depicting his life and times.

Marble Mountain Ski Area near Corner Brook has one of the longest ski seasons in eastern Canada. There are 26 runs, the longest of which is 3.2 km (2 mi.).

Port aux Basques Museum highlights maritime artifacts and old navigation instruments, including those from the *Caribou*, a ferry torpedoed in 1942.

The South Coast is dotted with a string of unique communities accessible only by boat. The boat passes deep fjords, vertical cliffs and plunging waterfalls before arriving at the snug harbours of some of the island's most picturesque outports.

Table Point Ecological Reserve, north of Gros Morne National Park, is a unique rock containing 470-million-year-old limestone and many well-preserved fossils.

Wittondale Pioneer Village, Bonne Bay, is a reconstruction of an early twentieth-century village. The site includes a restored turn-of-the-century house, general store, church, schoolhouse and barn.

Important Dates

1000	Vikings settle briefly at L'Anse aux Meadows.
1497	John Cabot arrives in the harbour at St. John's.
1501	Gaspar Corte-Real explores Hamilton Inlet.
1534	Jacques Cartier sails through the Strait of Belle Isle.
1583	Sir Humphrey Gilbert lands at St. John's and claims the land for Britain.
1610	John Guy establishes a small colony at Cupid's Cove on Conception Bay.
1614	The first Court of Justice is held in Trinity.
1662	The French establish a colony at Placentia.
1696- 1697	Le Moyne D'Iberville attacks and destroys a number of English settlements.
1713	France surrenders the island to Britain, but retains fishery rights on the French Shore.
1729	The first naval governor, Captain Henry Osborn, arrives from England.
1763	The Treaty of Paris places Labrador under the authority of the governor of Newfoundland.
1764	Moravian missionary Jens Haven makes his first visit to the Inuit of Labrador.
1805	The first post office is established in St. John's.
1829	Shanawdithit, the last of the Beothuk, dies.
1832	Newfoundland is granted representative government.

1855	Newfoundland becomes a British colony with responsible government.
1869	Newfoundland decides not to join Confederation.
1881	Construction of a railway begins on the island.
1892	A huge fire destroys much of St. John's.
1901	Marconi receives the first transatlantic radio transmission in St. John's.
1904	France gives up all claim to the French Shore.
1908	William Coaker founds the Fishermen's Protective Union.
1909	The first paper mill opens in Grand Falls.
1916	Hundreds of Newfoundlanders die in the battle at Beaumont Hamel in France.
1925	A second paper mill is opened at Corner Brook; Memorial College is founded.
1927	The Privy Council settles the Labrador boundary dispute.
1928	Lady Helena Squires is the first woman elected to the House of Assembly.
1931	Newfoundland becomes a self-governing Dominion.
1934	A bankrupt Newfoundland gives up Dominion status; a Commission of Government is put in place.
1939	The Second World War begins; more than 500 Newfoundland women serve in the armed forces.
1941	British Prime Minister Winston Churchill and American President Franklin Roosevelt

sign the Atlantic Charter at Quidi Vidi.

1948	The people of Labrador are allowed to vote for the first time; a referendum decides that Newfoundland will join Canada.
1949	Newfoundland and Labrador becomes Canada's tenth province; Joseph Smallwood is the first premier; Memorial College becomes a full-fledged university.
1953	Resettlement program begins.
1965	The Trans-Canada Highway is completed across the island.
1966-1974	The Churchill Falls hydroelectric station is built.
1974	Dorothy Wyatt is elected mayor of St. John's, the first woman to hold the position.
1979	Vast offshore oil fields are discovered at Hibernia.
1984	The Supreme Court of Canada rules in Quebec's favour in a dispute over profits from Churchill Falls; Micmac of the Conne river Reserve are granted Indian status under the Indian Act of Canada.
1985	An Arrow Airjet, chartered by the United States military, crashes in Gander as it takes off, killing 256 people.
1989	Investigation begins into charges of abuse at the Mount Cashel Orphanage for boys.
1990	Newfoundland opposes passage of the Meech Lake Accord.
1992	A moratorium is declared on the northern cod fishery.

Important People

Agnes Marion Ayre (1890-1954), born in St. John's; botanist; collected and made paintings of flowers indigenous to the province; published *Wildflowers of Newfoundland*

Selma De Lotbiniere Barkham (1927-), born in England; discovered documents on the Basque whaling station at Red Bay; responsible for the discovery of the *San Juan,* shipwrecked at Red Bay in 1565; awarded the Order of Canada in 1982

Robert Bartlett (1875-1946), born in Brigus; explorer; navigator; in 1908, guided American explorer Robert Perry to the North Pole

Emile Benoit (1913-1992), born in L'Anse-aux-Canards; taught himself to play the fiddle as a youngster, composed over 100 jigs and reels and recorded many of them; awarded the Order of Canada

David Blackwood (1941-), born in Wesleyville; printmaker and visual artist whose prints have been shown around the world; elected to the Royal Academy of Arts, 1975

Cassie Brown (1919-1986), born in Rose Blanche; writer; famous for her works about seal fishing and shipwrecks; *Death on the Ice* is her best-loved book

Johnny Burke (1851-1930), born in St. John's; singer, songwriter; poet; playwright; wrote hundred of ballads about Newfoundlanders and their way of life, many of which are still sung today

Lydia Campbell (1818-1904), born at Hamilton Inlet, Labrador; writer, considered the first published Labradorian; her diary was published in the *Evening Herald* in 1894

George Cartwright (1739-1819), born in England; explorer and chief trader off the coast of Labrador for 16 years; author of a three-volume journal detailing those years

Richard J. Cashin (1937-), born in St. John's; lawyer; politician; founding president of Newfoundland Fishermen Food and Allied Workers Union

William Epps Cormack (1796-1868), born in St. John's; explorer, naturalist; in 1822, with Micmac guide Joseph Sylvester, completed the first recorded walk across the interior of the island, then published a book on its wildflife; befriended Shanawdithit and recorded her accounts of Beothuk culture

John Crosbie (1931-), born in St. John's; lawyer; politician; cabinet member in Smallwood government; Conservative member of Parliament 1976-93; held several cabinet positions;

Agnes Marion Ayre

Emile Benoit

David Blackwood

Cassie Brown

Richard J. Cashin

John Crosbie

Craig Dobbin

Julia Salter Earle

passionate defender of Newfoundland

Craig Dobbin (1935-), born in St. John's; businessman; founder of Canadian Helicopter Corporation, the second largest commercial helicopter operator in the world with 52 locations in Canada and 10 elsewhere

Julia Salter Earle (1877-1945), born in St. John's; socialist and activist; first president of the Ladies Branch of the Newfoundland Industrial Workers Association; instrumental in winning the vote for women; one of the first women to run for public office

Alex Faulkner (1935-), born in Bishop's Falls; first Newfoundlander to play in the NHL; he and his brother George were famous hockey players of the 1960s; played with the Detroit Red Wings

Eugene Alfred Forsey (1904-1991), born in Grand Bank; author, professor, constitutional expert; a founder of the Co-operative Commonwealth Federation (CCF), he worked in the Canadian labour movement for 27 years; appointed to the Senate in 1970

John Gibson (1931-), born in India; came to Newfoundland in 1978; a world-acclaimed fish biologist, specializing in salmon, river ecology and environment protection

Edythe Goodridge (1937-), born in St. John's; freelance journalist; helped form the Newfoundland Historic Trust; has served as executive director of Newfoundland and Labrador Arts Council, curator of MUN Art Gallery, and Canada Council's head of visual and performing arts

Armine Gosling (1861-1942), born in Quebec; came to St. John's in 1882 to head Bishop Spencer College; president of Women's Suffrage League; founder and president of the Society for the Protection of Animals

Elizabeth Goudie (1902-1982), born in Mud Lake, Labrador; author of several works related to life in Labrador; frequent contributor to *Them Days* magazine; received an honorary doctorate from MUN in 1975

Wilfred Grenfell (1865-1940), born in England; missionary doctor; passionately committed to improving the lives of the poor, he established hospitals, nursing stations and orphanage-schools in Labrador and north-western Newfoundland; organized volunteers, raised funds and tried to help make the people self-supporting

Ray Guy (1939-), born in Arnold's Cove; humorist; writer; columnist in *Atlantic Insight* since 1979; witty and irreverent, his columns poke gentle fun at everything from his family, the CBC and politics to the rest of Canada; winner of the Stephen Leacock Medal for humour

Harry Hibbs (1942-1989), born on Bell Island; musician; moved to Toronto in 1962 where his legs were crushed in an accident; recorded 19 albums — 7 of which were gold

Mina Hubbard (1870-1953), born in Ontario; in 1905 she set out on an expedition through Labrador and produced the first useable map of the Naskaupi and George River systems; author of *A Woman's Way Through Unknown Labrador*

Percy Janes (1922-), born in St. John's; traveller; author; one of Newfoundland's most important fiction writers; his works reflect the confusion and anxiety of modern life along with a profound concern for the environment

Marilyn John (1951-), born on the Conne River Reserve, Bay d'Espoir; charted claims for aboriginal rights for the Newfoundland Micmac; became Band Chief in 1989

Kevin Major (1949-), born in Stephenville; author; he has written several acclaimed works for children and young adults including *Blood Red Ochre*, about the Beothuk, and *Dear Bruce*

Springsteen; has received several important Canadian book awards

Greg Malone (1948-), born in St. John's; actor-writer; solo performer and member of nationally renowned group CODCO; Gemini award recipient

Joan Morrissey (1935-1978), born in St. John's; singer; her albums, tours, wit and dedication helped carve out a niche for Newfoundland music; starred in the CBC show *All Around the Circle*

Joyce Nevitts (1916-), born in England; first director of MUN School of Nursing, 1965-73; author of *White Caps and Black Bands;* recipient of Canadian Volunteer Award in 1988 for her work with handicapped, hearing impaired and the aged

Paul O'Neill (1928-), born in St. John's; journalist; producer; director; author of *Spindrift and Morning Light* (poems) and several other books; produced over 2000 programs with CBC Radio; founding president of Newfoundland Writers Guild and Newfoundland Historical Society

Frederick Albert William Peacock (1907-1985), born in England; deacon in the Moravian Church; author of *The Labrador Inuit: Lore and Legend* and *Reflection from a Snowhouse;*

John Gibson

Mina Hubbard

Marilyn John

Greg Malone

Vera Perlin

Mary Pratt

Nancy Riche

Thomas R. Ricketts

produced an Inuktitut dictionary in 1945

Brian Peckford (1942-), born in Whitbourne; welfare officer; teacher; politician; Conservative premier, 1979-89; a strong defender of his province's rights

Vera Perlin (1902-1974), born in St. John's; president of the Newfoundland Association for the Help of Retarded Children, 1956-74, the first institution of its kind in St. John's; in 1967, she was named Newfoundland's Woman of the Century

Gordon Edward Pinsent (1930-), born in Grand Falls; actor, author, director; wrote *The Rowdyman* and starred in the film version; author and star of the television series *John and the Missus* and co-author of *A Gift to Last;* officer of the Order of Canada

Helen Fogwill Porter (1930-), born in St. John's; author of several books and co-editor of *From This Place: A Selection of Writings by Women of Newfoundland and Labrador;* received the Arts Council Lifetime Achievement Award in 1993

E.J.Pratt (1882-1964), born in Western Bay; poet; professor; famous for his evocative poetry about Newfoundland and his narrative poetry about Canadian heroic themes; won three Governor General's awards

John Christopher Pratt (1935-), born in St. John's; visual artist and printmaker; has garnered an international reputation for his stark, realistic paintings; designed Newfoundland flag

Mary Pratt (1935-), born in New Brunswick; visual artist; her paintings often involve domestic life, particularly things found in the kitchen, and are vibrantly realistic; *Red Currant Jelly* hangs in the National Gallery of Ottawa

Nancy Riche (1944-), born in St. John's; social activist; executive vice-president of the Canadian Labour Congress, president of the federal New Democratic Party

Thomas R. Ricketts (1901-1967), born in Middle Arm; soldier; pharmacist; received the Victoria Cross for bravery in the First World War, the youngest winner in the British army and the only recipient from the Newfoundland Regiment

Ted Russell (1904-1977), born in Coley's Point; writer; magistrate; MHA; author of several works humorously depicting provincial life; best known for his radio plays and stories about the fictitious outport, Pigeon Inlet

Doris Saunders (1941-), born in Cartwright; editor of *Them Days* magazine since its first edition in 1975, she has made an enormous contribution to the heritage of the Labrador people; awarded the Order of Canada

Tommy Sexton (1957-1993), born in St. John's; actor, revolutionary writer and originating force behind CODCO; recipient of a Gemini award

Shanawdithit (c.1801-1829), last survivor of the Beothuk people; her drawings and the stories she told are among the few records of her people's culture

Joseph Smallwood, (1900-1991), born in Gambo; journalist, broadcaster, politician; driving force behind the movement to have Newfoundland join Canada; first premier of the province, in power 1949-72

Geoff Stirling (1921-), born in St. John's; philosopher; student of Eastern religions; established the *Sunday Herald* in 1946; established CJON Radio in 1950

Georgina Ann Stirling (1867-1935), born in Twillingate; opera singer, known professionally as Marie Toulinguet, acclaimed for her performances at the Paris Opera and La Scala in Milan

Lynn Verge (1950-), born in Corner Brook; lawyer; politician; deputy premier, 1989, and founding member of the group that became the Corner Brook Status of Women Council

Clyde Wells (1937-), born in Buchans Junction; lawyer; politician; premier since 1989; strong defender of Canadian federalism

Fran Williams (1944-), born in Hopedale; activist; protector of Inuit culture; has made major contributions to Inuit communications network in Labrador

Wendy Williams (1949-), born in St. John's; social activist; president of the Provincial Advisory Council on the Status of Women; elected to St. John's City Council in 1990

Doris Saunders

Lynn Verge

Fran Williams

Premiers of Newfoundland and Labrador Since Confederation

Joseph R. Smallwood	Liberal	1949-72
Frank D. Moores	Conservative	1972-79
Brian Peckford	Conservative	1979-8
Thomas G. Rideout	Conservative	1989
Clyde K. Wells	Liberal	1989-

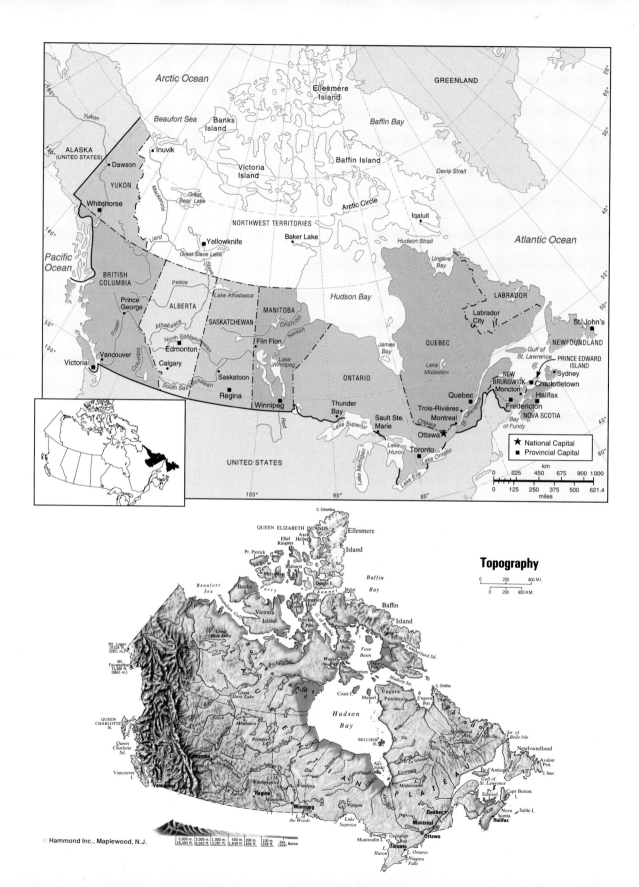

Arctic Ocean

GREENLAND

Ellesmere
Island

Beaufort Sea

Banks
Island

Baffin Bay

ALASKA
(UNITED STATES)

• Inuvik

Victoria
Island

Baffin Island

Davis Strait

• Dawson

YUKON

Whitehorse

Arctic Circle

Great
Bear Lake

Atlantic Ocean

Iqaluit

NORTHWEST TERRITORIES

Hudson Strait

• Yellowknife

• Baker Lake

Ungava
Bay

Great Slave Lake

Pacific
Ocean

BRITISH
COLUMBIA

LABRADOR

Peace

Lake Athabasca

Hudson Bay

Labrador
City

Prince
George

ALBERTA

Fraser

Athabasca

SASKATCHEWAN

MANITOBA

Churchill

Nelson

QUEBEC

NEWFOUNDLAND

St. John's

Edmonton

North Saskatchewan

Flin Flon

James
Bay

Lake
Mistassini

Gulf of
St. Lawrence

PRINCE EDWARD
ISLAND

Calgary

Vancouver

Victoria

Columbia

Saskatoon

Lake
Winnipeg

ONTARIO

NEW
BRUNSWICK

Sydney

Charlottetown

South Saskatchewan

Regina

Quebec

Moncton

Halifax

Red

Winnipeg

Thunder
Bay

Trois-Rivières

Montreal

Fredericton

NOVA SCOTIA

St. Lawrence

Bay
of Fundy

Lake Superior

Sault Ste.
Marie

Ottawa

National Capital

Provincial Capital

Lake
Huron

Toronto

UNITED STATES

Lake Michigan

Lake Ontario

Lake Erie

km

0   225   450   675   900 1000

0   125   250   375   500   621.4

miles

Topography

0   200   400 MI.

0   200   400 KM.

© Hammond Inc., Maplewood, N.J.

5,000 m. | 2,000 m. | 1,000 m. | 500 m. | 200 m. | 100 m. | Sea
16,404 ft. | 6,562 ft. | 3,281 ft. | 1,640 ft. | 656 ft. | 328 ft. | Level
Below

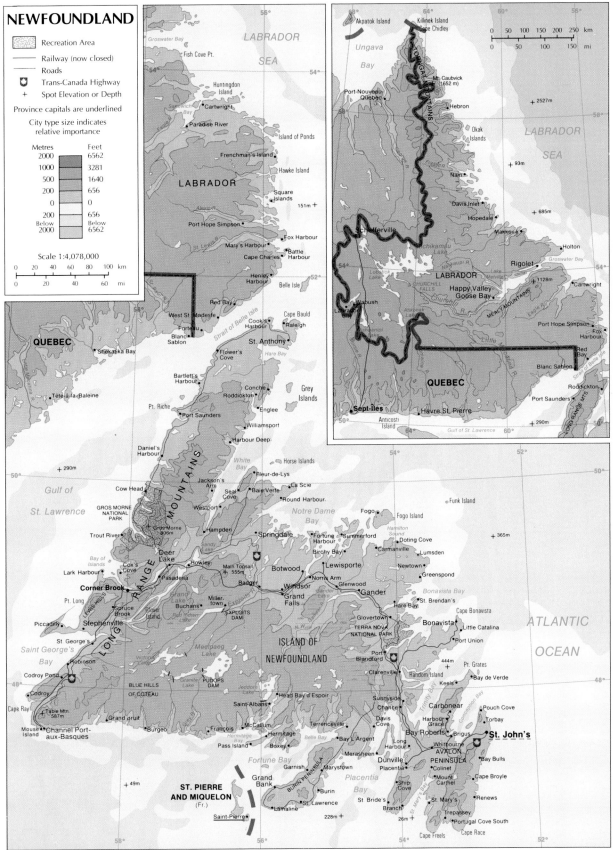

NEWFOUNDLAND

Recreation Area
Railway (now closed)
Roads
Trans-Canada Highway
Spot Elevation or Depth

Province capitals are underlined

City type size indicates
relative importance

Metres	Feet
2000	6562
1000	3281
500	1640
200	656
0	0
200	656
Below 2000	Below 6562

Scale 1:4,078,000

0 20 40 60 80 100 km
0 20 40 60 mi

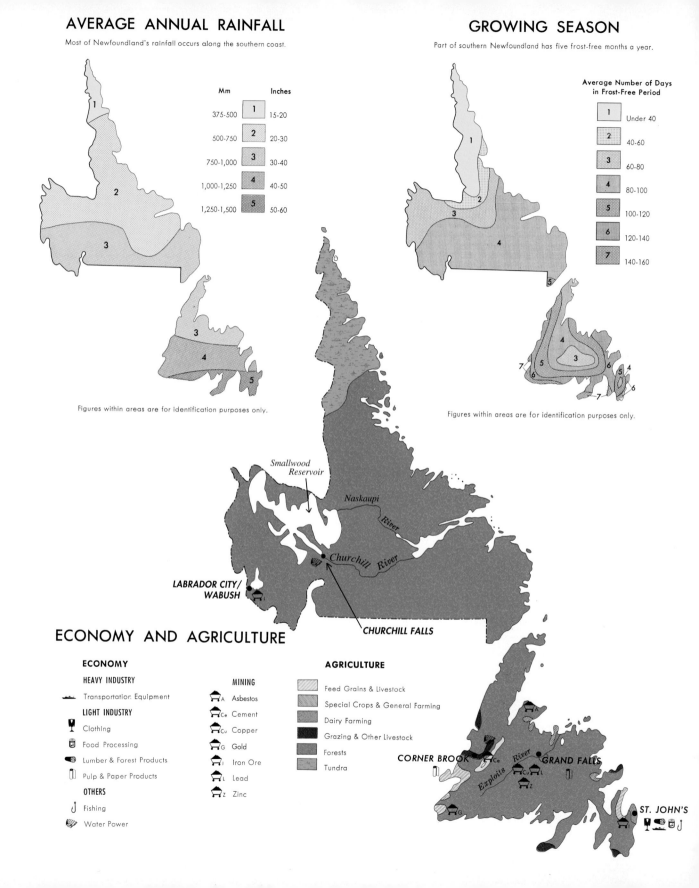

AVERAGE ANNUAL RAINFALL

Most of Newfoundland's rainfall occurs along the southern coast.

Mm		Inches
375-500	1	15-20
500-750	2	20-30
750-1,000	3	30-40
1,000-1,250	4	40-50
1,250-1,500	5	50-60

Figures within areas are for identification purposes only.

GROWING SEASON

Part of southern Newfoundland has five frost-free months a year.

Average Number of Days
in Frost-Free Period

1	Under 40
2	40-60
3	60-80
4	80-100
5	100-120
6	120-140
7	140-160

Figures within areas are for identification purposes only.

Smallwood Reservoir

Naskaupi River

Churchill River

LABRADOR CITY/ WABUSH

CHURCHILL FALLS

ECONOMY AND AGRICULTURE

ECONOMY

HEAVY INDUSTRY
- Transportation Equipment

LIGHT INDUSTRY
- Clothing
- Food Processing
- Lumber & Forest Products
- Pulp & Paper Products

OTHERS
- Fishing
- Water Power

MINING
- A Asbestos
- Ce Cement
- Cu Copper
- G Gold
- I Iron Ore
- L Lead
- Z Zinc

AGRICULTURE
- Feed Grains & Livestock
- Special Crops & General Farming
- Dairy Farming
- Grazing & Other Livestock
- Forests
- Tundra

CORNER BROOK

Exploits River

GRAND FALLS

ST. JOHN'S

Index

About the Author

Marian Frances White was born and raised in Newfoundland where she continues to live. She studied journalism at Carleton University in Ottawa, and since then has made her living as a writer and editor. She has published several annual agenda books featuring stories and historical information on the lives of women living in Atlantic Canada, as well as a book on artist Rae Perlin, *Not a Still Life*. Her most recent work includes a book of poetry and a film script.

Picture Acknowledgments

Abbreviations for location on page are, alone or in combination: T=Top, M=Middle, B=Bottom, L=Left, R=Right, I=Inset, BG=Background.

Front cover, 2-3, 4, 6, 8, 51, 77BR, 81, 97TR/MR, 101, 105BL, 111, 114, Malak/**Ivy Photo**; 5, 12, 34, 57, 62, 72, 97TL, 99TL, 100, 103, 107, George Hunter/**Ivy Photo**; 10L, 17BR, 28L, 47I, 52, 55BL, 56, 58R, 60B, 67BR, 69, 78L, 93T (etching 15" x 36" reproduced with permission of David Blackwood), 96BL/BR, 97B, 101I, 106, back cover, **Ivy Photo**; 10R, 33, 105BR, W. Lowry/**Visual Contact**; 12I, 121T, **Rose-Marie Kennedy**; 13, 14L, 65R, 95L, 99TM, 100I, 102TL/BR, 103R, © Barrett & MacKay/**Ivy Photo**; 13I, 108 (flower), Bill Ivy/**Ivy Photo**; 14R, 68, 96T, Wayne Sturge/**Whale Research Group**; 17L, 28R, 87TL/BR, 99B,102BL, 108 (bird), **Department of Tourism & Culture**; 17TR, **Bill Duffett**; 18 (C 17988), 21, 23 (C 28544), 26 (C 041605), 31 (C 3686), 36 (C 87698), 42 (C 5579), 55TL (PA 128080), 58L (PA 128004), 65L (PA 124429), 67BL (PA 128770), **National Archives of Canada**; 20, 25, 41, 74, **Metropolitan Toronto Library Board**; 39, **M5 Advertising and Destination Labrador**; 40 (both), 60TL, 106I, **Camille Fouillard**; 41B, **Michael Hockney**; 44, 108BG, Winston Fraser/**Ivy Photo**; 44I (both), 46, 50, 67L, 118B, 119MT, **Provincial Archives**; 47, **Ivy Collection**; 55TR, **Newfoundland and Labrador Hydro**; 55BR, 85R, **Department of Forestry**; 60R, 91BL, **Marian Frances White**; 75, **Department of Mines**; 77T, 102TR, Derek Trask/**The Stock Market Inc., Toronto**; 77BL, **SolidArt**; 78R, © Barrett & MacKay/**Department of Forestry**; 81I, **Marine Institute**; 85L, **Friends and Lobbyists of the Waterford River**; 87TR, **Courtesy Ron Hynes**; 87BL, **The McMichael Gallery**; 88, **Outport Designs, Carbonear**; 89L, 117MT, **St. John's Folk Art Council**; 89R, **Photo by Andrew MacNaughton**; 90L, **St. John's Day Committee**; 90R, © **SOLE**; 91T, **Courtesy Nicole Nogaret Dance School**; 91BR, 119MB, **Courtesy CODCO**; 93B, Jamie Lewis/**Newfoundland and Labrador Crafts Development Association**; 95R, **Helen Bidgood**; 96M, 99TR, 105, 113, **Bristol Communications**; 117T, **Courtesy Dr. Peter Scott/MUN Collection**; 117MB, 120MT, **Memorial University Art Gallery**; 117B, **Courtesy Christine Brown**; 118T, **Courtesy FFAW**; 118MT, Andrews-Newton, Ottawa/**Office of John Crosbie**; 118MB, © **Rostotski Studio**; 119T, **Gordon King**; 119MB, **East Coast Women and Words**; 120T, **Courtesy John Perlin**; 120MB, © **Photo Features Ltd.**; 120B, Centre for Newfoundland Studies Archives/**MUN Collection**; 121M, **Fran Williams**; 121B, **Courtesy Provincial Advisory Council on the Status of Women**